D0194124

In Defense of Affirmative Action

In Defense of
AFFIRMATIVE
ACTION

BARBARA R. BERGMANN

A New Republic Book
BasicBooks
A Division of HarperCollinsPublishers

Copyright © 1996 by BasicBooks,
A Division of HarperCollins Publishers, Inc.

Designed by Elliott Beard

Library of Congress Cataloging-in-Publication Data

Bergmann, Barbara R.
    In defense of affirmative action / Barbara R. Bergmann.
      p. cm.
    Includes index.
    ISBN 0–465–09833–9 (cloth)
    ISBN 0–465–09834–7 (paper)
    1. Affirmative action programs—United States.   2. Minorities—Employment—Government policy—United States.   I. Title.
HF5549.5.A34B47   1996
331.13'3'0973—dc20   95-40201
                                                        CIP

97 98 99 00 ❖/RRD 9 8 7 6 5 4 3 2 1

To the two white men I know best,

my husband Fred and my son David,

who want a world better than the one we have

Contents

Acknowledgments

Thanks are due to Robert Post, Harriet Baber, Fred Bergmann, Faye Crosby, Fred Graham, Mary Gray, Heidi Hartmann, Emily Hoffnar, Julie Nelson, Bernice Sandler, Air Force Lt. C. Smith, Sandra Tangri, and Carol Ullman, all of whom read parts of the manuscript in its various incarnations.

Some of the material in chapter 7 previously appeared in "Probing the Opposition to Affirmative Action," *Gender, Work, and Organization* 2, no. 2 (April 1995), and is reprinted with permission. The photograph on p. 140, © 1991 by the *Washington Post*, is reprinted with permission.

one

Thinking about Affirmative Action

When Bill Clinton was campaigning for the presidency in 1992 as the candidate of the Democratic Party, he promised to appoint a cabinet that "looked like America." At the time Clinton made his rather poetic promise, nobody, including his political enemies, spoke out against it. Nobody said that attempting to fulfill that promise would be a bad idea.

A cabinet that really looks like the American labor force would have six of its fourteen seats filled by white and minority women and two of its seats filled by minority men. As Clinton's cabinet selection process was approaching its end in early 1993, only two of the appointments had gone to women. Feminist organizations, concerned that women would again be restricted to the marginal role they had played in all previous administrations, urged publicly that more women be appointed. Women reporters at Clinton's news conferences kept asking him about it.

This pressure provoked an angry outburst from Clinton. He said that those pressing him to appoint more women were "playing quota games" with the selection process, implying in his response that he himself disapproved of quotas. The truth, however, was that Clinton did want to appoint more women than his predecessors had, and he had apparently decided that three was the number he wanted. Many reasonable people would call that "setting up a quota," since Clinton was trying to appoint women to a predetermined number of slots. At that point, with few vacancies left, the simplest and most practical way to ensure the appointment of a third woman was to earmark one of the remaining slots for a woman. That Clinton had done so became nakedly obvious when his first female candidate for the office of attorney general ran into trouble. He then put forward a second woman for the job and discarded her in turn when a problem arose. His third woman candidate was appointed and confirmed. She, like the other two, was obviously capable, qualified, and experienced. But by that time it was clear that Clinton had not been looking for the "best person" for the post of attorney general without regard to sex or race—he had been looking for the "best woman."

The Clinton cabinet episode raises questions that always arise when attempts are made to increase the gender and racial diversity in any group of employees. One fundamental question is whether diversity of sex or race or ethnicity in the cabinet was a worthy and important goal. How much harm would have been done if Clinton had appointed a cabinet consisting entirely or almost entirely of white males? He might simply have explained that each cabinet officer he appointed was, in his honest opinion, the best he could select from the wide range of candidates of both sexes and all ethnic and racial groups that he had considered. Would real harm have been done to the country's interests?

In thinking about that, we can note that presidents have always taken care to see that all geographic regions are well represented in the cabinet. Seeking that kind of diversity is not considered wrong; it is thought of as just being fair to all sections of the country. People in the West would be surprised and suspicious and hurt if the cabinet turned out to contain only people from east of the Mississippi. Clinton's selection of a cabinet that was markedly short of women and minorities would have done something far worse—it would have dealt a major setback to the pride and status of people in those groups. It would have strengthened the hand of those who think women, blacks, and other minorities do best in the jobs they have traditionally held and should stay there.

A second question is whether Clinton could have succeeded in assembling a reasonably diverse cabinet without setting up numerical goals by race and sex. Could he have avoided a cabinet that was completely or almost completely composed of white males without paying attention to the race and sex of the candidates as he made his appointments? There are good reasons to think that the answer is no. Dozens of superbly qualified and well-connected white males were available and competing for each cabinet position. A white male president can be expected to be most comfortable with advisers who are white males. Unless he disciplines himself by using a system of hiring goals for women and minorities, he may do the most comfortable thing and appoint only white males. President Clinton showed his leanings in this regard when he appointed his key White House staffers. They were chosen without publicity, and apparently without any effort at affirmative action. They all turned out to be white males, with one exception—a woman who was later replaced by a white male.[1]

Suppose, in appointing the cabinet, Clinton had chosen, one at a time, the person who appeared to him to be the best for each post, taking no special measures to find and include women and minorities and not worrying about appointing "too many" white males. How likely is it that there would have been much if any diversity by sex or race in his cabinet? Clinton really did have to mark out a seat for a woman if he was to shoehorn that third woman into the cabinet. The need to resort to such a potentially embarrassing method testifies to the low chance of achieving the degree of diversity he wanted without it.

A third question concerns fairness. Male candidates had been excluded in the search for an attorney general. The slot had been marked for a woman precisely for the purpose of fending off an otherwise nearly certain male appointment. If we focus on the situation of just that one excluded man, the initial reaction of many people would probably be that he had been dealt with unjustly and that the procedure that excluded him was wrong and should be abandoned. He had been subjected to "reverse discrimination."

Of course, exactly the same thing could be said about an easterner who had been excluded so that enough westerners might be fitted in. Yet nobody would make a point of that easterner's existence or have a moment's worry about the unfairness of that person's treatment. Perhaps fixing a race or gender imbalance provokes more worries about fairness than fixing a regional imbalance because the appointment of "too few" westerners would be considered only accidental, rather than a reflection of a deservedly low status. Everybody is willing to assume that the westerner appointed to achieve regional balance will be about as qualified as the easterner who might otherwise be appointed.

Efforts to increase women's low representation do generate resistance. The worry about the fairness of barring males from three of sixteen slots is an expression of the assumption that the women chosen must have been inferior to the men not chosen. In fact, that widespread assumption of women's basic inferiority and unsuitability for many roles is the reason women are most often excluded from those roles in the absence of a conscious effort to include them—in the absence of affirmative action. That assumption makes affirmative action indispensable if change is to occur.

Opponents say that the adoption of affirmative action has meant a shift from "nondiscrimination" to "minority preferences."[2] They are telling us that when affirmative action was adopted we went from a good and fair system to a bad and unfair one. By earmarking a certain number of the cabinet seats for women, Clinton did show a "preference" for women, although only in the case of the three seats. A few seats were also reserved for black and Hispanic men. For the remaining seats, no effort was made to interfere with the strong preference for white males in such roles.

Failing to establish a "preference" for women in those three seats might well have resulted in no women at all in Clinton's cabinet. "Nondiscriminatory" and "sex-blind" are two ways to describe a process that takes no special care to include women. "Allowing the strong preference for males to continue unchecked" is a more accurate way to describe it.

Another question raised by affirmative action is the potential harm to those intended to benefit by it. It is said that an employer who uses affirmative action to appoint people to jobs makes suspect the qualifications of all members of the targeted groups, and such suspicions are often cited as a potent source of grief and disadvantage to the intended beneficiaries. This issue does not appear to be relevant to cabinet officers, who are judged on their performance rather than on the factors that promoted their appointment. However, this is obviously a question that needs to be considered when we examine appointments to more ordinary jobs and when we consider college admissions.

In this book the main concern is the means, if any, that we should use to increase diversity of race and sex in all kinds of jobs.

Some attention is also paid to the attempts of colleges to increase diversity of race and ethnicity in their student bodies. The questions about affirmative action in those contexts are the same as those about the cabinet: How serious is our failure to achieve diversity? Could we achieve it by some means other than affirmative action? Does affirmative action promote fairness or the reverse? Does affirmative action harm its intended beneficiaries?

What Is Affirmative Action?

Affirmative action is planning and acting to end the absence of certain kinds of people—those who belong to groups that have been subordinated or left out—from certain jobs and schools. It is an insurance company taking steps to break its tradition of promoting only white men to executive positions. It is the admissions office at the University of California at Berkeley seeking to boost the number of blacks in the freshman class beyond a smattering by looking for a few black kids who may not have learned to do well on multiple choice tests but are nevertheless very smart. It is a lily-white all-male trucking company hiring a black female driver and then coping with the anger of the other drivers. It is the Detroit Police Department striving to overcome the obstacles that capable blacks and women experience in making sergeant. Affirmative action can be a formal program with a written, multipart plan and a special staff to carry it out, or it can be the activities of one manager who has consulted his conscience and decided to do things differently. The concept of affirmative action has been extended to ensuring that a share of government contracts go to minority-owned firms and to helping black groups or women's groups to buy broadcasting facilities.

Government has taken the lead in pushing affirmative action. The employers and schools with affirmative action plans may be public or private, but all have been mandated or encouraged by government regulations to achieve diversity. Nevertheless, there is no government agency that has closely monitored affirmative action activities and has cracked down on the noncompliant; the pace of affirmative action for the most part has been left to the discretion of individual workplaces and schools, whether private or public. Private companies with fewer than fifty employees are exempt from affirmative action regulations; they employ about one-third of American workers.[3] Larger employers are seldom if ever called to account for their staffing patterns by a government agency; the continuance of segregation almost never brings serious penalties. For example, the Ford Motor Company sells to the federal government and thus has been under a mandate to hire fairly for decades. Yet in 1992 only 4 percent of its managerial jobs were occupied by women; at many other large companies, 30 to 50 percent of managers performing similar functions were women.[4]

Thus, while the government officially promotes affirmative action, it is not an exaggeration to say that its application has been largely voluntary. As a result, desegregation of employment by race and sex has been uneven. While some public- and private-sector employers have made strides in increasing workforce diversity, many others have accomplished little or nothing. As we shall see in chapter 2, the condition of the American labor market suggests that much remains to be done. Abolishing, curtailing, or forbidding affirmative action anytime soon, particularly in employment, might abort further progress and cause the resegregation of some workplaces.

The Motives behind Affirmative Action

We can cite three major motives for affirmative action. The most obvious one is the need to make systematic efforts to fight the discrimination that still exists in many workplaces against African Americans, Hispanics, and white women. Exhortation against discrimination, which can be ignored, has not inspired much progress, nor have expensive lawsuits against a handful of discriminators—these can take decades to work their way through the courts. Affirmative action provides a series of practical steps for dismantling discrimination: rounding up promising candidates, getting rid of artificial barriers, outflanking influential people who do not want to see change, shoehorning capable candidates into positions not previously held by people of their race or gender, and grooming the best of them for larger roles.

A second motive for affirmative action is the desire for integration—for achieving racial and gender diversity in certain activities.

Diversity has positive value in many situations, but in some its value is crucial. To give an obvious example, a racially diverse community needs a racially diverse police force if the police are to gain the trust of all parts of the community and if one part of the community is not to feel dominated by the other part. While education and physical fitness are certainly aspects of "merit" in police officers, and while an appropriate floor on merit needs to be set and adhered to, efforts to get a corps of officers who are as educated and fit as possible should not be allowed to produce a police force that fails to include significant parts of its community. In such cases, it is legitimate to take account of what a candidate contributes to diversity.

A third motive for affirmative action is to reduce the poverty of certain groups marked out by race or gender. Those who advocate this reason for affirmative action are sometimes derided as wanting equality of results rather than equality of opportunity. The derision seems to arise from a belief that the high rate of poverty among blacks is of no interest whatsoever to anybody with any sense. However, the United States is now experiencing how dysfunctional and divisive the concentration of poverty in the African American community is.

Discrimination in the job market is an important cause of high poverty rates among U.S. children. It denies many single mothers, both black and white, access to jobs that would allow them to cover their health care and child care needs and to live at a decent standard. Their inability to keep their children out of poverty is a source of much present suffering and will lead to much grief in the future, as today's poor children mature and become one-quarter of America's adult population.[5]

Affirmative Action and Quotas

Opponents of affirmative action have been working hard for decades to make *quota* into a word that signifies something bad, wrong, indefensible. The measure of their success in demonizing quotas is that many people who favor affirmative action feel compelled to express assent to that view of quotas. They say that, of course, they too are against quotas, and that affirmative action and quotas are not the same thing.

Affirmative action plans, designed to get qualified women and minority people into jobs they have rarely if ever held, entail important activities that have nothing to do with quotas. The typical plan calls for efforts to get applications for each kind of job in reasonable numbers from qualified people from previously excluded groups. The office administering the plan looks at the process used to select candidates for hiring or promotion, trying to remove any source of bias. It tries to see that people from previously excluded groups are treated fairly and protected from harassment once they are on the job. Under an affirmative action plan, an employer may send supervisors—the employees who have a big say in hiring and promotion and whose past decisions have resulted in segregating jobs by race and sex—for training about racism, sexism, and sexual harassment and the laws and regulations against discrimination.

However, such activities are not all there is to affirmative action. The heart of an affirmative action plan is its numerical hiring goals, based on an assessment of the availability of qualified minority people and women for each kind of job. If progress is to be made toward those goals, some break with past practices is generally required. Those implementing the plan inevitably have to pay attention to the race and sex of appointees and exert pressure on or bypass those who have previously controlled the selection process. It is this aspect of affirmative action that draws the accusation that affirmative action is the same thing as a quota system.

There may be cases in which pressure to achieve a numerical goal is unnecessary—as when the appearance of the first good black or female candidate in the list of applicants for a previously segregated job generates an enthusiastic response among those doing the selecting. But there are many situations in which a female candidate or a nonwhite candidate, regardless of qualifications, has little chance of getting the job without such pressure. Those who say that affirmative action means "quotas" are talking about those goals and that pressure to fulfill them.

Advocates of affirmative action have argued that the numerical goals of affirmative action programs are not quotas because these goals are provisional, not hard and fast. The goals can be reduced or abandoned if no suitable African American or white female candidates can be found.[6] This defense does not really address the issue that makes affirmative action goals objectionable to many people. They want hiring and selection systems that reward merit and are fair to all candidates. They worry that racial or gender goals, whether rigid or soft, are incompatible with such systems.

The cause of honest debate over the costs and benefits of affirmative action is probably served if those defending affirmative action acknowledge that such programs do have quotalike aspects. The argument that has to be made to justify affirmative action goals is that under present conditions the merits of black and female candidates are habitually overlooked, that we cannot achieve diversity without numerical goals, and that having them does less harm than not having them. Of course, that defense is premised on the belief that the absence of certain kinds of people from certain places in our society is not due to their lack of competence, that such absences are an important source of grief and harm for many, and that those absences ought to be repaired if the process of doing so is tolerable on ethical grounds.

What Affirmative Action Tries to Cure

From the heat of the outcry against affirmative action one might imagine that quotas for women and blacks are common and assiduously being filled in every workplace. However, the truth is that the pattern of the absence of minority people and women from many kinds of jobs persists almost untouched in many work-places, despite the substantial progress made in others. We continue to see white male monopolies in most of the high places and many of the not-so-high places in American society: in the higher management of almost all business firms, in the upper ranks of government service, and among firefighters, surgeons, over-the-road truck drivers in the rigs cruising American highways, skilled crafts workers on almost any building site, and tenured professors in most subjects at all universities. Change is occurring, but it is slow and halting.

There would be no question of a further need for affirmative action if it were not true that for many jobs the race and sex of the person chosen can be predicted with a high degree of certainty. If a particular job has always gone to men, then a woman is unlikely to be appointed without special pressure to locate good women candidates and to overcome the resistance to hiring them. Similarly, if a job has always been occupied by white people, a white person is overwhelmingly likely to be chosen for a vacancy, absent a conscious effort to find a suitable black person and award him or her the job.

Despite the time that has elapsed since passage of the Civil Rights Act of 1964 outlawing discrimination, thousands of American workplaces continue to offer jobs that seem permanently earmarked for those of a particular race or sex—either for a man or for a woman, either for a person with light-colored skin or a person with dark-colored skin. Traditional ideas about what kind of person can be competent in which job remain strong and still influence selection.

Very few jobs are as well integrated by sex and race as the position of cabinet officer. Much publicity accompanies the cabinet choices, but most vacancies are filled by a selection process that operates behind closed doors. There are lots of jobs available in the United States that a woman would not have a hope of obtaining, no matter how competent she is. Similarly, there are lots of jobs that bright African American job seekers could do well and want to do but are not seriously considered for. Many studies by economists and sociologists suggest that there is still much discrimination going on in the United States—against white women on account of their sex, against African Americans on account of their race, and against Hispanic people on account of their ethnicity. Black and Hispanic women get a double dose.[7] We look at some of those studies in chapter 2.

Much of the poverty, social disorganization, welfare dependency, and crime our country suffers is rooted in discrimination against people based on race and sex and in the deprivation and feelings of exclusion, hopelessness, and resentment it causes. If we could make progress in overcoming discrimination on the job, many of our social problems would ease. The miasma of racial distrust and resentment that fuels much crime and misbehavior and motivates the flight from racial integration in housing and public schools would start to dissipate.

Any realistic person knows that people who are not both white and male occupy a very small share of the satisfying, well-paying jobs. From the 100-member U.S. Senate (92 percent male, 99 percent white, through 1996) to the nearest construction site, it is obvious that white men continue to predominate in the best positions by a wide margin. From data entry clerks to retail cashiers and cleaning staffs, it is obvious that blacks and women predominate in the boring, dead-end, ill-paid positions. Families that do not include a white man have a high chance of suffering extreme deprivation. Of children under six, only 8 percent of those with a white man in their family were poor in 1992, while 48 percent of those without a white man were poor.[8]

In this country, social status and respect are almost entirely derived from the job one holds. The rarity of blacks and women in the better jobs and their predominance in the worst jobs contribute to the widespread attitude—still expressed openly these days, although less commonly than in the past—that all blacks and all women, even those who have achieved good careers, have blemished status and are unworthy of full respect. Right-wing talk radio provides the most overt expression of disrespect these days—Rush Limbaugh recently labeled a woman college teacher "a professorette"—but disrespect turns up in many other places. The low status of blacks and women on the job translates into a lack of respect when they try to get mortgages or to buy cars. It puts them at a disadvantage in social interactions, in the justice system, in the physician's office, in their treatment by the police, in the legislation and implementation of public policy, in the decisions of medical researchers about who to include in their studies. Affirmative action is not just about improving the flow of wages to those whose earnings have been reduced by discrimination. It is also about putting them in a position where they can hold their heads up as normal citizens.

Contrasting Views of What Needs to Be Done

The controversies about affirmative action stem from disagreements about the interpretation to be put on the current degree of exclusion and about what kind of actions, if any, should be taken to get rid of it. Those who believe that affirmative action is necessary and desirable think that there are white women and African Americans of both sexes who could perform well in jobs that, at present, they rarely hold. They see the social problems stemming from exclusion by race and sex as intolerable. They view the near-monopoly that white males maintain of many jobs as the result of custom, stereotypical thinking, old-boy networks, and plain discrimination. Advocates of affirmative action do not think that the command "Just don't discriminate" will accomplish much, and they see little chance of any but the slowest progress in eliminating the white male monopoly without affirmative action.

Others look at the same society and see something quite different. They see a system of assigning jobs based on merit. This assignment process has its occasional lapses, but by and large it is run fairly. Its prizes are most often awarded, as they should be, to the best—the talented, the hardworking, the well-prepared, the ambitious. Adherence to that system gives us, they think, our best chance of overcoming any lingering discrimination and eliminating the influence of race or sex in the selection process. Opponents of affirmative action believe it is a terrible mistake to compromise the principle of such a system for an increase in racial and sexual diversity in the short term. They see affirmative action leading to the imposition of a hateful balkanization of the job market—a division of spoils, with each distinguishable group raucously demanding its share.

Some opponents of affirmative action deny that there is much if any discrimination and think that the labor market is already quite fair, or that it would be if we got rid of affirmative action programs. Their diagnosis of the situation is that women and minority people generally are not as capable and do not strive as hard as white men, and so white men win out in the competition for the best jobs because they are the best applicants. They feel that blacks and women are already just about as successful as they deserve to be, perhaps more so given their abilities and the efforts they make.

The opponents of affirmative action say that when and if more African Americans and women acquire the right qualifications and a single-minded willingness to devote themselves to succeeding, they will get more of the better jobs. In the meantime, they do not deserve more of them, and their exclusion does not need to be remedied. For those who hold this point of view, the numerical goals that affirmative action prescribes are worse than unnecessary; they create injustice and inefficiency.

Among the opponents of affirmative action are some who, like the proponents, believe that the domination of the best positions by whites and males has had highly regrettable consequences for the whole society, and they would like to see that domination end. However, they believe that affirmative action is not the right remedy because it does more harm than good. Instead, they would rely on other means to increase the diversity of those in the better jobs, such as lawsuits to get rid of outright discrimination. Like other foes of affirmative action, they think the exclusion of women and African Americans results mostly from their objectively poor qualifications, and they favor vigorous public action to improve those qualifications. They advocate better elementary and secondary education for the disadvantaged and policies to improve family life.

Anyone of the opinion that the current system of hiring and promotion is fair enough, and that the inequalities that result from the present system are something we can and should live with, would conclude that remedies like affirmative action are unneeded and pernicious. An essential step in deciding whether affirmative action is a good or a bad idea is making a judgment as to whether we presently have a system that is by and large fair.

If it turns out, on examination, that the job market is still stacked against blacks and women, that they are overlooked and slighted not rarely, not just in the past, but now, often, and systematically, then both our laws and our values demand that something be done about it. Once we are at the stage of saying that something needs to be done, we can consider whether affirmative action should be part of the program we adopt.

Affirmative Action and Efficiency

The usual assumption, of both its foes and friends, is that affirmative action does cause some loss of efficiency because of the relaxation of the practice (supposedly in force in the absence of affirmative action) of picking the "best" candidate for each vacancy. That assumption is not always correct. Affirmative action lowers efficiency in some cases, and can raise it in others. Where there has been discrimination and care is taken to find good candidates from previously excluded groups, a properly operated affirmative action program may well result in the appointment of people who do better than those who would otherwise have been chosen. Affirmative action may enlarge the field of candidates and should eliminate selection procedures that screen out candidates for irrelevant reasons. For that reason, it may benefit some white men who, under previous criteria, would not stand a chance of being hired or selected.

A favorite tactic of the foes of affirmative action is to ask, "Would you like to be operated on by a surgeon chosen through affirmative action?" Those asking the question assume that the answer has to be no. Almost all the surgeons in the United States are white males. The absence of affirmative action in the surgical field by no means guarantees that the most qualified person is always selected. Gross bias is apparently common. Highly skilled women surgeons at the Stanford Medical School, at Children's Hospital in Washington, D.C., and at New York City's Columbia Presbyterian Hospital have in recent years protested being treated by male colleagues in ways both biased and disrespectful.[9]

A lot of bad surgery is performed, and some of those currently excluded from training might well do better than some who are currently included. A greater effort to recruit and foster talented women and black men in surgical residencies and to eliminate the harassment and discouragement they apparently suffer might pay off in improved surgical services rather than poorer ones. The use of numerical goals to pressure those who train surgeons to find and enroll promising black and female medical school graduates might well be necessary. Without that pressure, those who are comfortable with the white male near-monopoly in the field will continue to make decisions ensuring that almost all new surgeons are white males.

When whole groups are shut out, the highly talented individuals among them are lost. Among the monarchs remembered as outstanding in fostering their people's well-being, women figure far out of proportion to the total number who have been allowed to reign. Queen Elizabeth I of England, Queen Christina of Sweden, and Catherine the Great of Russia are all remembered as more hospitable to modernizing forces and far less wasteful of their countries' resources in warfare than were their male counterparts. Had rules of monarchial succession not favored males, the history of the human race might be a happier one. In more modern times, women heads of government have performed as effectively as their male counterparts.

Sometimes in a group of finalists for a previously segregated job no one candidate is head and shoulders above the rest. If some of the finalists are minority males or women, then appointing one of them should not, on average, lower the quality of appointees. But sometimes the best of the candidates from previously excluded groups are judged (and let us assume judged honestly and correctly) to be appreciably lower than the best white or male candidates. In such cases, searching further for better candidates may be indicated, or a training program might be instituted. A decision to allow a seemingly second-rate minority candidate to join the second-rate white males already on the job may work out, but clearly, the better the minority candidate, the less chance for significant trouble. Taking on a worker who looks unable to do or learn the job is a virtual guarantee of trouble down the road. No affirmative action plan requires that this be done.

Employers have big incentives to avoid a slapdash attitude toward the quality of the person chosen: "We're under pressure, so let's just find anybody of the right race and sex." They cannot afford to ignore quality any more than a president can in choosing his or her cabinet. They have to live at least for a while with the person chosen. Bad appointments can be very costly, whether in the cabinet, on the bridge of the *Exxon Valdez,* or in the cab of a truck on an interstate highway.

Affirmative action plans cannot be operated properly 100 percent of the time. There are bound to be some misapplications, that is, some appointments of atrociously inappropriate people. But plenty of mistakes are made even in situations where affirmative action programs are not in effect; plenty of white men are hired by mistake. With or without affirmative action, selecting people is not a well-developed science; incompetents do get hired and promoted, and inadequate students do get admitted. No human policy is immune to misapplication. But those of us who favor affirmative action must acknowledge that it may be especially prone to misapplication; thus, we must also endorse probationary periods and systems in which employers can easily fire for cause.

Issues of Fairness

For many who are upset by the idea of affirmative action, fairness is the key issue. They believe that the only fair system is one that puts the candidate judged most qualified into each vacancy. In those workplaces where black people have been excluded from jobs at which they could perform well, instituting an affirmative action plan removes one possible source of unfairness—the rejection of all black candidates, regardless of their qualifications. If a black candidate then appears whom everybody agrees is head and shoulders above all of the white candidates, ending the segregation by hiring that person poses no problems of fairness to any white. Such cases are the easy ones.

The hard cases are those in which the best black candidate appears amply qualified, but is not the one who has been judged the "best" of the current crop of candidates. Is it fair, under an affirmative action plan, to hire that person, and to pass over a white candidate who has been judged the "best"? If that is to be avoided, integrating the workplace would have to be delayed until a black candidate could be found who is not merely capable of doing the job well, not merely as good or better than many of the whites previously hired, but unquestionably superior to all the other current candidates. Given the possible bias in the process of judging (which in the past had allowed the segregation to persist), that might never come to pass.

Some might say that in those hard cases fairness and justice are best served by putting an immediate end to segregation by giving a chance to a highly acceptable black candidate. Others would say that fairness to the "best" candidate overrides all other considerations, and requires that the employer put off ending the segregation for as long as it takes to find that black candidate who will be judged to be the "best." In deciding which side to come down on in these hard cases, we have to balance the value of bringing segregation to a quick end with the value of avoiding violations of a (perhaps imperfect) merit system.

That violations of the merit system occur regularly for purposes other than bringing race segregation to an end—purposes such as helping a nephew or a friend, or taking on someone who will help the sports team—also needs to be taken into account when thinking about the hard cases. When such violations occur, fairness to the displaced "best" candidate is seldom an issue. As we have already noted, geographic balance is routinely sought when political appointments are made, and religious balance is considered as well. When a university gives preference in admission to an applicant who might strengthen the tennis team or is the child of an alumnus, grades and test scores are given less than usual weight in the decision. However, little resentment seems to be stirred by such decisions, even among those directly affected in a negative way. The appointments to the post of attorney general of President John F. Kennedy's brother and President Ronald Reagan's undistinguished personal attorney raised little negative comment.

It causes no adverse comment when large and important businesses, such as the W. R. Grace Company, the Washington Post Corporation, and the New York Times Company, place at their head the son or son-in-law of the majority stockholder or of the previous head. No protest is made that the company is acting unfairly to a better-qualified nonrelative who might otherwise have gotten the position. Nor is there any complaint, even from the stockholders, that the company's performance will be degraded by its failure to find the most qualified person. But if the *New York Times* attempts to ensure that it has blacks among its reporters and editors, then resentments arise. That some departures from choosing the "best" are accepted with no complaint at all, while departures made for the purpose of reducing the exclusion of African Americans or women are complained of bitterly, is something that bears thinking about.

We are told by opponents of affirmative action that we have to choose between equality of opportunity (without affirmative action) and equality of results (with affirmative action); they imply that the former is more fair than the latter. But our actual alternatives may be quite different. If discrimination remains widespread, then equality of opportunity in the workplace may not be achievable without a stiff dose of affirmative action. If the present capabilities of many women and African Americans are subpar, then well-run affirmative action programs, which avoid putting people into roles for which they are unfit, will not produce equality of results anytime soon. As I shall argue, the real choice is between a continuation of gross inequality of opportunity (if affirmative action is abolished) and a slow move toward more equality both of opportunity and result (if affirmative action is kept and strengthened).

The sense of grievance about the supposed unfairness of affirmative action is partly based on the belief that it has produced a huge rise in the fortunes of blacks and a huge decline in the fortunes of whites. The passionate campaign carried on against affirmative action by right-wing politicians conveys the message that affirmative action plans are widespread and have effectively moved those who had previously done poorly—blacks in particular—not simply into parity but into a privileged position. Supreme Court Justice Antonin Scalia, who opposes affirmative action, refers to white males in one of his opinions as a "disfavored group."[10]

The fact is, of course, that in the labor market white males retain largely intact the highly favored position they had in 1964, the year employment discrimination by race and sex was made illegal. In 1994, among those working full-time, pay for white non-Hispanic males was 49 percent higher than pay for other labor force participants.[11] Differences in skill levels account for some of this pay difference, but nowhere near all of it.[12] Segregation on the job by race and sex remains a common pattern. Opening access for all to the job enclaves that are now the preserves of white males would take a far more rigorous application of affirmative action techniques than has yet occurred. It would take the introduction of vigorous affirmative action programs into the many workplaces where they have been absent or ignored.

Alleged Hurt to Beneficiaries

Among the opponents of affirmative action and numerical goals are some African Americans whose main complaint is that the policy undermines respect for its intended beneficiaries. They claim to be stigmatized by the common assumption that they did not make it on their own and, furthermore, could not have. Stephen Carter, a black professor at Yale Law School who sees both benefits and costs to affirmative action, says that he is forced to live in a box with a label on it, that says, "WARNING! AFFIRMATIVE ACTION BABY! DO NOT ASSUME THAT THIS INDIVIDUAL IS QUALIFIED!"[13] This perception is especially galling to those who believe they could have made it on their own. Others, who are not so sure that they could have made it without affirmative action, must have mixed feelings.

In thinking about this issue, we have to ask whether African Americans would be a less stigmatized group if there were fewer black undergraduates at Yale, fewer black Yale graduates, and fewer black members of the Yale faculty. We also have to ask about those doing the stigmatizing. Has affirmative action created derogatory feelings about blacks in people who would otherwise have had perfectly friendly feelings toward them? Or would those who stigmatize the blacks at Yale, citing affirmative action, have found some other reason to run them down? Moreover, what is the evidence for all this extra stigmatizing?

Balancing the Good and the Bad

Deciding whether affirmative action is worthwhile policy involves balancing the good against the bad: we must weigh the good and the bad results of keeping (or stepping up) affirmative action versus the good and the bad results of abandoning the modest number of vigorous affirmative action plans now in operation. While affirmative action may offer the possibility of important gains, it can have important disadvantages.

Like all "human engineering," affirmative action is difficult to implement effectively; the very fact that so many oppose it as vociferously as they do and feel that their interests are hurt by it increases that difficulty. Unless its management is in skilled and dedicated hands, affirmative action is easily bungled or sabotaged. Like painful surgery, affirmative action can be legitimately advocated only as a means of improving a bad situation. We do not want to use surgery if the patient is not really sick, if a less radical remedy will work, if the pain and disability caused by the surgery are likely to be worse than the effects of the illness, or if the surgery is likely to be ineffective in treating the patient's illness.

In surgery, one person suffers the costs and reaps the benefits. However, in affirmative action, the benefits and costs go to different sets of people. When goals and timetables are implemented, some people are denied advantages they might otherwise have had because others are able to share in the advantages they previously monopolized. This means that we must pay particular attention to the problem of fairness between individuals.

The purpose of affirmative action goes beyond improving the position of individuals or of previously deprived or unsuccessful groups. Those who favor affirmative action programs believe that such programs can change the nature of our whole society. They hope that affirmative action will help us move toward a fairer society—one in which people are less disabled in the competition for jobs by race or sex than they now are. This view must seem paradoxical to those who believe affirmative action to be the acme of unfairness and an invalid injection of race- and sex-based criteria into selection processes. Those of us who favor affirmative action need to demonstrate that in fact it can lead to less unfairness and eventually to less attention to race and sex in hiring, promotions, and school admissions.

If we achieve a more fair society than the one we now have, even those people who are currently in favored positions are likely to receive some material and psychological benefits. They would live in an environment with less crime, less welfare dependency, less hatred, less anger, less injustice, and more civility. Those of us who feel some guilt over the present situation would feel less. These benefits to all of a fair society should go some way toward compensating some of those who are currently best favored for reducing the degree of ascendancy they now enjoy.

Here, then, are the key questions about affirmative action, and the answers to them I am going to advocate:

- Are African American women and men and white women in our society badly hobbled by continuing discrimination practiced against them? *Yes*.
- Does the discrimination against them that currently exists justify a remedy like affirmative action? *There is good evidence that it does.*
- Could other remedies be substituted? *No one has proposed any others that promise to do the job.*

- Is it unfair to use affirmative action to exclude the whites and men who would normally be chosen to be hired? *If the alternative is to continue to exclude competent blacks and women, it is not.*

- Are the benefits of affirmative action worth the costs? *In many situations, they are.*

- Are numerical goals and timetables the same thing as quotas? *It is not unreasonable to say so.*

- Are goals and timetables indispensable? *Yes.*

two

Is Discrimination a Thing of the Past?

Pollsters surveying people about their attitudes toward affirmative action frequently ask, "Do you think blacks or women should receive preference in hiring and promotion to make up for past discrimination?" This wording encourages respondents to assume that discrimination has ended and is no longer an important problem. Respondents to one such poll, when asked to comment on their answers, spoke of discrimination that had occurred "100 years ago" and said that such ancient history did not justify "preferences" in the present.[1]

As we shall see in this chapter and the next, there are good reasons to believe that discrimination by race and sex is not a thing of the past. Those under the impression that discrimination ended a long time ago are simply mistaken. However, they are right about one thing: our need for affirmative action depends not on what happened 100 years ago but on the situation in the labor market today.

In the United States, about one million jobs are filled in an average month.[2] If women and African Americans have access to the jobs currently being filled, then affirmative action programs are unnecessary and we should dismantle them. On the other hand, if their access to a significant portion of the jobs they could do well is severely limited, then something ought to be done to break down that barrier. In this chapter, we look at the issue of fair access for African Americans and women. We will see that, in spite of the progress toward fair access that has been made since the 1960s, we are not even close to having achieved a labor market in which a candidate's sex and race don't matter. In many workplaces, a candidate's sex and race are still noticed when job assignments are made. That's how women continue to get segregated into "women's jobs" and African American people into "black jobs."

Opponents' Views of the Labor Market

Some opponents of affirmative action go so far as to claim that there has never been a time since the Civil Rights Act was passed when labor market conditions needed rectification that might have justified affirmative action. For example, Richard J. Herrnstein and Charles Murray, authors of *The Bell Curve* (1994), suggest that blacks already had achieved nondiscriminatory access to professional and technical jobs around 1964, the year discrimination was outlawed by the Act, and nondiscriminatory access to clerical jobs by 1967, just three years later.[3] Herrnstein and Murray argue in effect that African Americans are unfitted by their genes for any better jobs than they had in the sixties, and that their progress since then has been unwarranted and perhaps should be reversed. Anyone familiar with conditions at the time the Civil Rights Act was passed knows that this position is ludicrous. In the early sixties, a regime of strict and total apartheid in the South continued to be enforced by violence. Blacks throughout most of the South could be killed with impunity for being "uppity," that is, for anything from owning too fancy a car to trying to register to vote. Most jobs throughout the country were segregated by race. The largest occupation for black women was household servant; the largest occupation for black men was laborer.[4]

Other, more realistic, opponents of affirmative action acknowledge that discrimination against African Americans and women was severe before 1964 and that it did not instantaneously cease with passage of the Civil Rights Act. They imply, however, without evidence, that at some (unspecified) time discrimination effectively ceased in this country. Affirmative action has been splendidly effective, according to this line of argument, and solved the problem of discrimination. But it has outlasted its time of usefulness. Today affirmative action gives blacks and women an unfair advantage.

Yet another group of opponents, mostly conservative blacks, present a totally different argument. They claim that affirmative action has not helped blacks at all; on the contrary, it has severely hurt them, as evidenced by the deteriorating condition of black families in the inner city. Affirmative action has injured African Americans by making them believe a falsehood—that they are all victims of white oppression. This belief has made them resentful and removed their incentive to work hard and compete like other Americans.[5] This argument suggests that blacks encounter no problems in the labor market that could not be overcome by better behavior on their own part.

Most of the debate over affirmative action has been carried on in racial terms. White conservative politicians critical of affirmative action have been silent on the gender angle, perhaps in fear of alienating women voters. Some black men feel that efforts on behalf of white women divert energy from improving conditions for African Americans, whose problems, in their view, merit higher priority. There is not even agreement that discrimination against women, if it exists, should be ended. A prominent federal judge (often mentioned during Republican administrations as a worthy Supreme Court nominee) has argued that the legal prohibition of discrimination against women is undesirable. It may help women with jobs, but hurts housewives, who have an interest in their husbands' wages being as high as possible.[6]

There are, of course, those who claim that women's position in the labor market is and has always been exactly what women wish it to be. Men would not dream of oppressing their sisters, wives, and mothers in the labor market. In this view, it is not sex discrimination that keeps women out of "men's jobs" but the free desire of most women to give priority to home duties.[7] As we shall see, there is good evidence that white and African American women do suffer considerable discrimination on the job because of their sex.

The Evidence on Wages

In judging the conflicting claims about the state of the labor market, it is useful to start by looking at how much change has actually occurred. Chart 2.1 shows the weekly wages of those who worked full-time in the years 1967–95, corrected to eliminate the effect of inflation.[8] The inflation-corrected wages of white men have been on a downtrend since the mid-1970s. However, white men have not lost their superior position in the labor market: a substantial gap remains between their wages and those of white women and black men and women. Given the slowness of change in the labor market, as shown in chart 2.1, that gap will not close anytime soon.

Modest reductions have been made in that gap since 1967. Black men's wages were 69 percent of white men's in 1967. By 1976 their wages had risen to 79 percent of white men's. Since

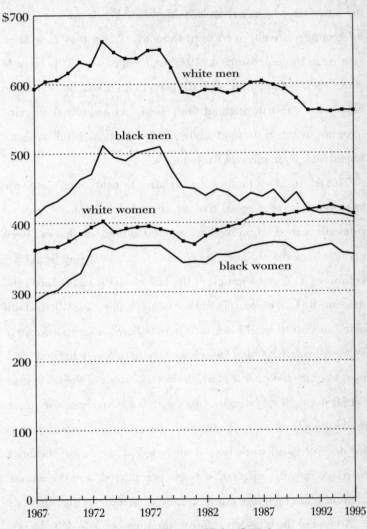

Chart 2.1

Weekly Wages by Sex and Race in 1995 Dollars

white men

black men

white women

black women

Based on data from the U.S. Bureau of Labor Statistics.

then, they have been losing rather than gaining ground on white men. The loss of manufacturing jobs, some of them unionized and thus relatively well-paying, has hit both white and black men, but the latter have been particularly hard hit.[9] White women gained no ground on white men until the early 1980s; they have been gaining in the years since. In 1995 their wages were 73 percent of white men's, compared with 61 percent in 1967. Black women have made gains throughout the period, but recently their gains have not matched those of white women. In 1995, black women's wages were 63 percent of white men's.

The fall in black men's wages relative to white men's over the last twenty years suggests that whatever help they have received from affirmative action has been modest at best, and has not been enough to counterbalance the effects of their buffeting from market forces. The globalization of the labor market has reduced the demand by U.S. employers for the labor of the less skilled—both black and white—and black men have suffered disproportionately. While affirmative action has allowed some college-educated black men to enter the middle class, the deterioration of the labor market for non-college-educated black men has been disastrous. It has made their lives increasingly precarious; their decreased chances for decently paid work have contributed to the fall in the black marriage rate, the increase in single parenthood, and the recruitment of black men into crime and the drug trade in the inner city.

An end to the long-term slide in the wages of less-skilled workers would obviously be highly desirable for its own sake. That slide is having many unfortunate effects, of which the worsening climate for affirmative action is only one. The drastic social and political consequences of a continuation of that slide can easily be foreseen. There is no way to attack it that is guaranteed to improve matters and that does not pose formidable political difficulties. That said, it has to be realized that there is never an easy time to make efforts at reducing the disadvantages of groups that have been subordinated. Allowing those efforts to stall or go into reverse would exacerbate our social and political problems.

Not all of the gap in wages between white males and other workers is due to discrimination in the workplace; a wage gap may also reflect the differences between workers in education, experience, and other factors, such as residence in low-wage regions. Statistical techniques allow us to measure how much of the gap is due to nondiscriminatory factors and to remove their effect from the gap, leaving a "residual gap," which is a better approximation of the extent of wage loss due to current workplace discrimination.[10] Table 2.1 presents two estimates of the residual gap between white males and other groups, based on two different sources of information on conditions in the labor market. Neither source tells the whole story, but taken together, they give us an approximate idea of the size of the penalty that current discrimination exacts from each group.

In table 2.1, one set of estimates of the residual gap derives from information on people's wages collected by the National Longitudinal Survey of Youth (NLSY). The NLSY tells us about

Table 2.1

**Two Estimates of the Effect of Discrimination
on Yearly Wages, 1991**

	Based on Census Data (ages 18–65)	Based on NLSY Data, Including Measures of Cognitive Ability (ages 26–33)
black men	$4,145	$1,522
black women	7,294	3,393
white women	6,903	3,539

Figures based on U.S. Bureau of the Census data were calculated by the author from current weekly wages of full-time workers, assuming 52 weeks of pay. Those derived from the NLSY are based on hourly wages of persons employed full time, and assume an average of 40 hours of pay per week and 52 weeks of pay. These estimates do not include losses to blacks due to their higher unemployment rates.

the workers' sex and race, as well as their education, age, experience, area of residence, and scores on a test of cognitive skills.[11] The second, considerably larger set of estimates of the residual gap derives from Census Bureau data. A reasonable estimate of the effect of discrimination on the earnings of each group probably lies somewhere between these two sets of figures, both of which pertain to 1991. The NLSY-derived estimates are too low because they cover only workers in the age range 26–33. Much of the effect of discrimination shows up after age 33. In their thirties, some white men are being promoted into well-paid and high-status jobs, whereas women and African Americans who, in their twenties, were placed in dead-end jobs miss out on such promotions for the most part. If the figures derived from the NLSY are too low, the figures derived from the Census data are too high. That data set, unlike the NLSY figures, contains no information on individuals' cognitive skills. Part of the difference in pay between blacks and whites is legitimately due to their differences in this regard: a higher proportion of blacks attended poor schools as children and their families and neighborhoods had fewer resources to help them develop their skills.[12]

The true penalties of discrimination suffered by average full-time black and female workers lie somewhere between the high and the low figures shown in table 2.1: about $3,000 a year for black men and $5,000 for black and white women. These estimates, though only approximate, suffice for our purpose, which is to decide whether discrimination effectively ended some time in the past. The evidence on earnings from the Census Bureau and the NLSY suggests that discrimination is still very much alive.

The Extent of Job Segregation

The wage gaps we have been discussing arise from a pervasive and obvious workplace practice. Anyone passing a building site will notice that all the construction workers are men. Anyone enrolled at a sizable university is likely to find that among the school's 150 or so tenured professors of chemistry, economics, and political science, none are black and perhaps two or three are female. In a newspaper photograph of the crowded trading floor of the New

York Stock Exchange or of one of the commodity exchanges, we see dozens of people, all of them men, all of them white.

There has been some progress: since the 1960s, African Americans and women have been gaining representation in some occupations to which they rarely had access in the past.[13] However, the presence of blacks and whites, and men and women, in the same occupational groups does not mean that they all are on an equal footing when they are being considered for vacancies. Even when men and women have very similar jobs, they seldom are coworkers. Men who wait on tables generally work in expensive restaurants where the tips are high and no women are hired. Women tend to work in the cheaper restaurants, with no male colleagues.

Thanks to the work of the sociologist Donald Tomaskovic-Devey, we have systematic statistical information about the extent of segregation by sex and race among coworkers in the same job for the same employer. In 1989, he asked a sample of North Carolina workers about the race and sex of their coworkers who did the same kind of work they did and had the same job title.[14] He found that blacks and women were not excluded from any broad categories of work (see table 2.2).[15] However, a considerable majority of people worked exclusively with people of their own sex. Jobs in which 100 percent of the incumbents were male or 100 percent were female together accounted for 70 percent of all jobs. In another 16 percent of all jobs, segregation by sex was not total but nearly so. Only 14 percent of the respondents held jobs in which

Table 2.2

Occupational Segregation by Sex and Race

	jobs held by women (percent)	workers who work only with people of own sex (percent)	jobs held by blacks (percent)	workers who work only with people of own race (percent)
Managers	41.3	84.7	10.7	91.5
Professionals	59.2	50.3	17.4	48.6
Technicians	50.5	61.0	20.6	52.6
Supervisors	44.6	86.5	8.0	86.4
Sales workers	53.7	59.0	17.3	54.4
Clericals	81.8	81.1	16.6	65.0
Craft workers	10.6	75.9	21.2	51.3
Operatives	53.6	73.5	31.9	35.8
Laborers	53.5	71.6	30.9	40.0
Service workers	51.3	51.6	36.0	54.4
All jobs	52.6	70.0	21.6	55.7

Donald Tomaskovic-Devey, *Gender and Racial Inequality at Work: The Sources and Consequences of Job Segregation* (Ithaca, N.Y.: ILR Press, 1993). Data refer to a 1989 survey of workers in North Carolina. In this context, "worked with" means "shared a job title with."

males and females worked together in numbers approximating their share in the workforce.[16]

The North Carolina survey found that segregation by race is less strict than segregation by sex. Still, a majority of the respondents

(56 percent) worked in jobs that were totally segregated by race. Another 30 percent worked in jobs that were almost totally segregated. Only 15 percent of the jobs were shared by blacks and whites in numbers roughly proportional to their workforce presence.

The North Carolina survey results are broadly consistent with the findings of the Labor Department's Office of Federal Contract Compliance Programs (OFCCP), the federal agency that visits government contractors to inquire about their compliance with non-discrimination requirements. The agency found that in 1994–95, 75 percent of the employers it checked were in substantial non-compliance.[17]

The extremity of the segregation by race and sex found in the North Carolina survey is made clearer if we think about segregating workers a different way—by birthday. Birthdays of workers are about evenly split between the first half of the year and the second. Suppose we go into a workplace, pick out a particular job title, and survey the birthdays of all the workers holding that title. We would certainly be surprised if we found that all of them had birthdays in the first half of the year. In fact, if nobody is paying attention to birthdays when people are assigned to jobs, we would expect to observe such extreme segregation by birthday in a group of ten coworkers less than one time in a thousand. Suppose that a particular workplace has not just one birthday-segregated job title but many. In some kinds of jobs, all the workers were born between January and June; in others all have a birthday between July and December. If groups that are totally segregated by birthday were to account for 70 percent of the jobs in a workplace, we would have little difficulty in concluding that when people were assigned to jobs in that workplace, their birthdays were being noticed.

In fact, with that degree of segregation, it would be obvious that their birthdays had far more influence on their job assignment than their talents and potential for doing good work in the various kinds of jobs around the workplace. Segregation by birthday would not necessarily rule out all consideration of merit and qualifications; some jobs allotted to those with January–June birthdays might require above-average education, and some July–December jobs might also. However, where birth date is a major factor in placing people in jobs, the importance of merit in making those assignments is certainly greatly reduced.

Suppose that the jobs occupied by people with birthdays in the first half of the year have considerably higher salaries than the jobs occupied by those born in the second half. In fact, suppose that the lowest salaries paid in January–June jobs are higher than the highest salaries paid in the July–December jobs assigned to people of equivalent education. Suppose the duties assigned to people in the July–December jobs are more routinized, more boring, and harder to perform, and that the chances for promotion are far lower than in the January–June jobs. We would have to conclude that the purpose of the system goes beyond separating people according to their birthdays—specifically, that the system was designed to bring great advantages to those with birthdays in the first half of the year and to visit great disadvantages on those with birthdays in the second half. In the parlance of sociologists, the July–December people would constitute a subordinated group.

If the subordination of the July–December people were a new phenomenon, we would expect them to be as well educated, devoted to their work and careers, and productive as people born in the first half. If, however, their subordination both in and out of the workplace had gone on for quite a long time, it is reasonable to assume that differences in outlook and education would have developed between the two groups.[18] Such differences would certainly be cited (especially by those who benefit from the status quo) to justify the inferior position of the July–December people in the workplace. Moreover, the wisdom of establishing an affirmative action program to place some qualified July–December people into January–June jobs would be decried.

People of color and women have, of course, been subordinated groups for a long time; as a result, differences in education, abilities, skills, and attitudes between them and white males have developed. These differences, however, are not so stark as to justify—"on account of merit"—the extreme degree of segregation that the North Carolina survey reveals. The least capable white available is not inevitably going to be better in a certain job than the most capable black available. The least capable man available will not always do better than the most capable woman available. Since differences in the qualifications of women and men, and of blacks and whites, cannot account for the extreme degree of segregation the surveys turn up, we have to conclude that those who make job assignments are paying a great deal of attention to race and sex when they decide who is allowed to have which job. Qualifications such as education and ability are not ignored, but if a worker is female, not a lot of attention is paid to her suitability for jobs traditionally assigned to males with her education and ability. If a worker is African American, his or her suitability for a job traditionally assigned to similarly educated and skilled whites may not be noticed.

The purpose of affirmative action is to reduce segregation by race and sex in the workplace. Obviously, much of the segregation that affirmative action was designed to eliminate is still present. The argument that affirmative action programs have already accomplished so much that we no longer need any programs of this (or any other) type in the workplace cannot seriously be made by anyone who has examined the evidence of what is currently going on in the workplace.

Those who want to abolish affirmative action pretend that the result would be a system in which sex and race are not noticed when job assignments are made. The data on segregation by sex and race show that in many workplaces affirmative action has not been implemented, or at least not vigorously enough to have enabled more than a few blacks to have white coworkers, or more than a few women to have male coworkers. In those workplaces, race and sex are being noticed, but for the purpose of continuing to segregate people. Ending affirmative action would not put an end to the notice taken of race and sex in many workplaces when people are assigned to jobs. It would put an end to the effort to reduce segregation.

The Evidence from Lawsuits

Lucky Stores, Inc., a West Coast grocery chain, agreed in 1993 to pay nearly $75 million in damages to women who had been denied promotion opportunities and another $20 million to set up and run affirmative action programs.[19] The women had been denied full-time slots, and the relatively small group of women in management jobs had been segregated into certain departments (bakery and delicatessen) marked off as dead end. The managers of these departments received lower pay than other managers. One of the women whose complaint sparked the suit had worked at the cash register for twenty-one years. When her teenage son came to Lucky and worked beside her, he was offered training opportunities that had been denied to her. Suits alleging similar employment practices have been filed against Safeway Stores and several other grocery chains.

The facts of the Lucky Stores case were strikingly similar to the facts in a 1972 suit against Giant Foods, a Washington, D.C.–area grocery chain. That suit was settled, with the company under order until the late 1980s to remedy the problems. However, a 1994 tele-phone survey to ascertain the sex of managers by department revealed that in the twenty years since the suit, very little integration of managerial positions had been accomplished.[20] Meat cutting, a skilled trade requiring apprenticeship, had been maintained as an all-male specialty. Bakery managers, still overwhelmingly female, continued to receive lower salaries than other department managers, almost all male. The cost of remedying the bakery managers' relatively low pay would have amounted to a few dollars an hour per store; the fact that their pay had not been increased raises questions about the symbolic significance of low pay to those in control. Giant's history illustrates the stubbornness of discrimination problems and the difficulty of fixing them when management is indifferent or opposed to change. A successful lawsuit may give the particular complainants some recompense but leave the underlying situation unchanged. The supermarket cases also show the complicity of some unions in maintaining segregation by sex and women's lower pay.

A recent claim of racial discrimination against the Shoney restaurant chain listed 211 Shoney officials against whom there was direct evidence of discriminatory behavior. Employment applications were color-coded by race. Blacks were tracked to kitchen jobs so that all employees in the dining area would be white. The case began when two white managers complained that they had been pressured by their supervisors to limit the number of black employees, and that they had been terminated when they resisted the pressure. The case was settled out of court for $65 million. Kerry Scanlon, an attorney for the black plaintiffs, said, "This was going on while the Bush Administration and others were telling the country that in the area of civil rights, the major problem was quotas and unfair protection for blacks. The quota that African Americans are most familiar with in employment is zero."[21]

Evidence Based on "Testing" the Job Market

So far, in reviewing the labor market situation for women and blacks, we have been looking at their treatment on the job, that is, where they are placed and what they are paid. We need also to look at their ability to land jobs. An important aspect of the labor market disadvantage suffered by African Americans is their high unemployment rate. People are counted as "unemployed" in government statistics only if they are actively looking for work. In good times and bad, unemployment rates for African Americans are twice as high as those for whites. The problem is particularly acute for eighteen- to nineteen-year-old black people, who suffer unemployment rates above 30 percent.[22] When they leave school, it is very hard for them to find jobs, and when they lose a job, they are typically in for a long spell of unemployment before landing the next one.

The results of a recent research project reveal the extent of discrimination against young black men in hiring and give an insight into the connection between that discrimination and their high rate of unemployment.[23] The Urban Institute assembled pairs of young men to serve as "testers." In each pair, one tester was black, the other white. Entry-level job openings were chosen at random from the newspaper, and a pair of testers was assigned to apply for each opening.

The researchers made the pairs of testers as similar as possible, except with regard to race. Testers were matched in physical size and in the education and experience they claimed to have. An attempt was also made to match each pair in openness, energy level, and articulateness. The testers were actually college students, but most of them posed as recent high school graduates and were supplied with fictional biographies that gave them similar job experience. They were put through mock interviews and coached to act like the person they were paired with to the greatest possible extent. The testers were then sent to apply for low-skill, entry-level jobs usually filled by young high-school graduates in manufacturing, hotels, restaurants, retail sales, and office work. The job titles ranged from general laborer to management trainee. The testers were instructed to refuse any job offered them so that the other member of the pair could have a chance at it.

The black testers posing as job seekers were carefully coached to present qualifications apparently equal to those of their white counterparts. In reality they were all, black and white, excellently qualified for the jobs they applied for. The Urban Institute researchers found that the young white men were offered jobs 45 percent more often than the young black men. This result clearly reveals that some employers were not treating male minority job seekers equally with white males of similar qualifications.

The same researchers paired white Anglo testers and Hispanic testers who were fluent in English.[24] Again, the pairs of young men were matched to minimize the differences between them; the only apparent differences were the slight accents, somewhat darker complexions, and Spanish names of the Hispanic testers. The Anglos received 52 percent more job offers than the Hispanics.

Why Hasn't Affirmative Action Been More Effective?

The continuing high levels of discriminatory segregation in the nation's workplaces indicate that the task of improving access for women and minorities to all jobs for which they are qualified has by no means been accomplished. But why has affirmative action, which has aroused so much resentment on the part of white men, not done more to mitigate the effects of white male privilege? Is it true that affirmative action has not worked?

One obvious answer is that there are many workplaces where affirmative action has not been seriously implemented, where it has not been given a chance to work. Serious implementation of affirmative action is difficult, riles many people, and requires major behavioral changes by those who will make such changes only grudgingly. A serious effort to change may well prove disruptive, at least for a time, to a firm's personnel and operations. Many white people are angry about affirmative action, so opposition to a company's affirmative action plan can be expected.[25] Some of that opposition may come from the most valued and experienced employees, who are likely to be older white males. As a result, many firms are not going to make the effort that a successful affirmative action program requires unless they have top executives devoted to expanding opportunities for women and minorities or they are given a vigorous push by government.

Unfortunately, the OFCCP, the main government agency pushing affirmative action in the workplace, is understaffed, has few effective ways of encouraging compliance, lacks vigor, and has probably been poorly managed. Firms doing more than $50,000 worth of business with the federal government are required to report annually to the OFCCP their utilization of women and minority workers by major occupational group, and to compare that utilization with the availability of such workers. Firms are also required to have an affirmative action program with numerical goals and timetables for eventually utilizing these workers roughly in accordance with their availability.[26]

The OFCCP might have mounted a vigorous and well-targeted program to promote integration by race and sex. Since it is not limited to responding to complaints, as the Equal Employment Opportunity Commission (EEOC) is,[27] it can take on a proactive role. The OFCCP could choose to concentrate on the most egregious offenders among the large corporations, where the most impact might be made. However, that potential impact has been largely unrealized. The OFCCP's 1995 budget of $59 million and its staff of 918 provide minuscule resources for its task of supervising nondiscrimination in the 150,000 workplaces of federal contractors, which employ 28 million people, one-quarter of the nation's workforce. It makes about 4,000 compliance reviews a year, a rate at which it could investigate each workplace in its purview once every 38 years.

While the OFCCP has probably been somewhat more influential in changing corporate practices than the EEOC or the individual plaintiffs who have brought lawsuits charging race or sex discrimination, it has nevertheless been of quite limited effectiveness. Its main sanction is the debarment of a corporation from the approved list of federal contractors. Only forty-one firms have been debarred since 1972, out of the thousands whose long-term performance has been unsatisfactory. As negligible as the rate of debarment has been during Democratic administrations, debarment virtually ceased during the Reagan-Bush era.

Debarment is too severe to be used very often. A particular defense contractor may be the only source of a product the Pentagon wants. In addition, the debarment of a very large corporation would exact considerable political costs. Of the companies debarred since 1972, only four have been large corporations: Prudential Insurance, Firestone, Uniroyal, and Timkin Roller Bearing. All were debarred during the Democratic administration of Jimmy Carter. None of those debarments lasted very long; all four companies were reinstated within three months.[28]

We can judge the effectiveness of the OFCCP by looking at how well large government contractors have integrated their workforces by major occupational group. Table 2.3 shows the share of managerial and crafts jobs held by women and African Americans at a group of large government contractors. Note that companies report employment to the EEOC and the OFCCP only by broad occupational category; the figures do not tell us about segregation at the level of specific jobs. The North Carolina data showed that segregation at that level is pervasive, even in workplaces where broad job categories are integrated.

The figures on the utilization of women are relatively easy to interpret, because women are almost half of the workforce in all localities. Table 2.3 shows that different industries treat women very differently, and that within industries, companies differ considerably. Overall, the automobile industry has made very little use of women managers, but within that industry, General Motors has almost three times as many women managers as Ford does. In the oil business, Mobil and Atlantic Richfield have twice as many women managers as Union Oil. Manufacturers of food products, whose customers are mostly women, have done relatively little to allow women into management roles; within that industry, George A. Hormel and Company is an outstandingly bad performer. On the other hand, women are well represented among managers at financial firms and banks.[29]

All of the firms listed in table 2.3 have affirmative action plans. There is no obvious reason why their utilization of women managers differs so broadly. Many managerial functions are similar from one industry to another, and women are now well represented among business school graduates everywhere in the country.

Table 2.3

Women's and Blacks' Share in Managerial and Crafts Jobs
at Selected Large Corporations, 1992

Company	total employment	women's share		blacks' share		popu-lation
		managers	crafts	managers	crafts	
Mobil Corp.	39,709	15.2%	4.7%	6.0%	15.0%	17.8%
Atlantic Richfield Co.	19,941	18.9	4.0	3.6	7.3	10.6
Exxon Corp.	42,012	10.7	6.4	5.9	14.9	21.0
Union Oil Co./DBA Unocal	9,683	8.3	2.7	3.8	9.3	11.4
Geo. A. Hormel & Co.	8,304	4.1	6.4	1.2	9.1	8.4
Tyson Foods Inc.	45,999	16.4	17.3	7.8	11.7	12.6
Borden Inc.	25,047	12.1	13.6	3.6	18.8	12.7
Campbell Soup	25,967	19.3	12.4	3.4	10.5	10.5
Gerber Products Co.	10,455	27.3	5.8	2.3	3.2	10.5
H. J. Heinz Co.	16,737	27.6	12.3	2.2	5.7	9.1
Archer Daniels Midland Co.	10,920	6.2	1.9	2.9	9.7	13.5
Dow Chemical Co.	28,223	9.6	2.3	3.5	7.1	10.2
E. I. DuPont De Nemours & Co.	87,320	9.3	6.9	5.4	14.2	16.1
Monsanto Co.	21,303	15.9	3.2	5.0	9.1	19.0
Union Carbide Corp.	19,567	8.6	4.9	4.0	12.3	12.3
USX Corp.	45,798	30.4	2.1	4.4	14.4	15.6
Aluminum Co. of America	33,592	10.4	4.7	5.2	6.0	8.6
Apple Computer Inc.	8,404	33.1	10.0	2.4	0.0	6.5
Digital Equipment Corp.	53,559	25.7	4.2	4.6	2.0	8.5
IBM Corp.	203,812	21.7	25.5	7.8	10.2	13.2
UNISYS Corp.	40,240	15.5	7.1	3.0	5.2	12.3
Chrysler Corp.	88,614	7.8	2.3	8.7	11.3	16.6
Ford Motor Co.	140,780	4.4	1.6	8.6	9.5	18.1
General Motors Corp.	380,222	11.6	3.2	10.2	8.1	15.4
Boeing Co.	143,949	12.9	8.4	2.5	5.2	6.1
General Dynamics Corp.	61,339	5.8	7.8	3.2	7.9	8.9
McDonnell Douglas Corp.	87,471	9.5	13.0	4.0	15.0	12.3
Delta Air Lines Inc.	76,364	24.9	14.3	6.8	9.7	18.1
Southwest Airlines Co.	11,688	39.1	1.1	6.8	2.5	12.5
United Airlines Inc.	76,781	20.2	1.8	8.9	7.3	14.3

Table 2.3 cont.

Company	total employment	women's share		blacks' share		
		managers	crafts	managers	crafts	population
Federal Express Corp.	80,633	24.8%	2.3%	14.8%	9.3%	22.6%
A.T.&T.	136,176	45.2	7.7	10.6	5.6	16.6
MCI Communications	24,516	33.5	40.5	9.3	11.1	19.2
Nynex Corp.	22,711	40.0	7.6	4.9	2.8	5.1
Southern New England Telephone	11,125	63.3	12.0	12.8	5.4	10.8
Southwestern Bell	52,537	40.9	13.2	11.1	8.6	13.8
American Electric Power Co.	21,495	5.4	2.5	3.1	5.3	9.1
Florida Power Corp.	5,836	12.0	2.3	3.6	10.0	9.0
Ohio Edison Corp.	6,271	3.3	1.1	2.4	6.1	8.1
Potomac Electric Power Co.	5,123	15.3	1.3	18.4	28.2	26.6
Hewlett Packard Co.	54,107	25.3	3.4	2.0	2.1	5.4
Xerox Corp.	62,850	26.7	15.9	10.3	10.5	13.3
May Department Stores Co.	121,007	59.9	42.4	6.8	8.8	13.2
Sears Roebuck & Co.	405,628	37.4	4.1	8.2	11.2	13.6
Kroger Co.	141,114	30.1	15.0	7.6	9.4	17.5
Safeway Stores Inc.	77,876	30.4	26.6	4.1	6.3	9.5
Marriott Corp.	185,943	41.0	26.9	8.0	18.0	14.0
McDonald's Corp.	93,990	46.0	20.0	16.9	3.1	13.5
Bank America Corp.	93,402	61.2	4.8	5.5	2.9	8.4
Chase Manhattan Bank NA	27,271	42.5	1.7	7.8	7.5	18.2
Chemical Banking Corp.	38,357	44.4	16.1	11.3	21.0	22.0
Citicorp	42,709	41.5	5.1	7.0	7.0	16.6
Salomon Inc.	6,501	20.5	0.0	3.6	5.2	19.9
Wells Fargo Bank	31,253	66.1	0.0	7.5	16.7	7.6
National Medical Enterprises	51,078	59.0	23.3	4.4	8.0	12.4
Hospital Corp. of America	69,745	68.9	20.3	5.1	17.0	16.0
Humana Inc.	62,819	67.7	4.0	7.4	21.1	14.6

Figures compiled by the author using EEOC and OFCCP data.

In examining different companies' utilization of African Americans, the proportion of blacks in the population in the areas where the companies have their facilities, shown in the table's last column, must be taken into account. The differences in the utilization of blacks as managers shown in table 2.3 between McDonald's and the other retail businesses listed cannot be explained away that way, however. Companies differ in their toleration of segregation in their individual units. In the Boston metropolitan area (7.3 percent black), where many NYNEX facilities are located, 2,213 people were employed at one location in 1992; only 38 of them were African American. In a number of smaller NYNEX facilities in the Boston area, African Americans had only 1 or 2 percent of the jobs. Among one such facility's 116 employees, none were black. Southern New England Telephone Company, on the other hand, had substantial numbers of blacks in all of its facilities in urban centers.

What the company data confirm is that the OFCCP has done very little enforcement. Firms have been allowed to do pretty much what they feel like doing. In the private sector, affirmative action has been largely voluntary. Some firms have made progress, but others that have chosen not to do very much have not been called to account. A rational management of the OFCCP would have targeted the laggards such as Ford and NYNEX for close attention.

Overall, the verdict must be that government enforcement of prohibitions against discrimination and encouragement of integration have made some positive difference in corporate behavior, but that in many workplaces the government impact has been limited or nil. Perhaps the major impact of government affirmative action programs has been to familiarize the management of large corporations, if not the population at large, with the idea that no race or sex group has a legitimate monopoly on any set of jobs, and that a corporation that allows any jobs to be monopolized by white males looks bad.

As bad as the record of some larger firms is, progress has been even slower or nonexistent in most smaller firms. In small firms, the informality of procedures leads to continued recruitment from segregated sources, such as friends and relatives of the firms' own employees.[30] There are 6.2 million places of work in the United States, excluding government agencies. Of these, 6.0 million have fewer than 100 employees; these small workplaces employ 56 percent of those working for private employers.[31] A program intended to hasten the end of segregation by race and sex in such workplaces would have to emphasize the education of their managers and customers rather than enforcement through sanctions. Government sanctions should obviously be concentrated on the larger firms. Integration of the larger firms would provide a seasoned and experienced workforce balanced by race and gender, and some of them would eventually be employed in the smaller firms.

Has affirmative action failed? To come to that conclusion, we would have to see evidence of widespread efforts at earnest implementation of affirmative action plans thwarted by a lack of suitable candidates to fill the goals, the incompetence of those hired to fill them, the incompetence of program administrators, or the obstruction of those who oppose integration. From firms that have made special efforts to implement affirmative action, such as Xerox, Procter & Gamble, Rohm and Haas, Motorola, Dow Corning, GTE, Nabisco, and Northwestern Mutual Life, we have not heard reports of debilitating problems of this sort.[32]

A far more likely conclusion from the evidence we have reviewed is that the federal government has not been vigorous or skillful in promoting the implementation of affirmative action plans and policies. It has concentrated on ensuring that each federal contractor has an affirmative action plan somewhere in its files and a poster announcing its nondiscrimination policy on an employee bulletin board somewhere on its premises. (The Brookings Institution, where I worked for a time, had the poster in its poorly lit basement garage, where very few blacks or women had the privilege of parking.) Some firms have pushed affirmative action, but many firms have not yet changed their hiring and promotion practices to any significant degree.

A skeptic might argue that if affirmative action programs have not yet provided us with a labor marketplace in which women and African Americans have fair access to jobs they can do, such programs never will. With conservative politicians stoking the public's anger against affirmative action, the outlook is poor for a more vigorous implementation of affirmative action than we have had up to now. The appointment of more Supreme Court justices in the mold of Antonin Scalia and Clarence Thomas could doom its survival even as a program undertaken voluntarily by private employers.

Historically, the United States has had periods of regression in racial matters. Under President Woodrow Wilson, black employees were rooted out of the federal government and theaters and restaurants in Washington, D.C. were resegregated. We could regress again. Yet a majority of Americans do want to live in a country that is fair. In a national survey, high school seniors were asked whether they agreed or disagreed with the statement, "Maybe some minority groups do get unfair treatment, but that's no business of mine." Of those responding, 77 percent of female seniors and 60 percent of male seniors disagreed.[33] It is no longer clear that we will continue our slow move toward establishing the fairness in employment that these young people profess to want.

How Exclusion Occurs

As we have seen, more than three decades after the passage of the Civil Rights Act, segregation by race and sex continues to be the rule rather than the exception in the American workplace, and discrimination still significantly reduces the pay and prospects of workers who are not white or male. Some employers recruit applicants in ways that look fair but unintentionally produce biased results. In other workplaces, blacks and women are consciously kept out of certain jobs. Chapter 2 presented the evidence that many U.S. workplaces continue to practice discriminatory exclusion. This chapter explores how they do so.

The Hiring Process

Let's look at what happens when there is a vacancy for a waiter in an expensive restaurant that has never hired anyone but white men for that job. The restaurant publicizes the vacancy—in a newspaper ad, through an employment agency, or by asking current employees to spread the word. Some applicants are then interviewed, and the applicant deemed most promising by the persons making the hiring decision is given the job. How does it happen that no blacks and no women ever get such a job? Is their exclusion due to discrimination or to something else?

We can be quite sure that such an outcome does not occur merely by chance. Of the people who make their living as waiters, white men comprise about 15 percent of the total; therefore, 85 percent are from other groups. Suppose that, over its entire history, this restaurant has hired 150 waiters as new jobs opened up and as some waiters quit or were fired. Suppose further that this restaurant was choosing waiters from all of the job seekers available for this kind of work rather than from a pool of white males only. The chance that 100 percent of the waiters chosen would come from a subgroup of 15 percent of the job seekers is less than one in a million. An all-white-male crew of waiters does not happen by accident. Something is systematically ensuring that only white males are hired as waiters in this restaurant, something that systematically bars women and minority males from being hired.

Perhaps no blacks and no white women would ever want to take a waiter's job in this restaurant; therefore, they never apply, and that is why the restaurant never hires any. But is such a predisposition against taking a job in this restaurant likely? Why would the many experienced black waiters and waitresses and experienced white waitresses avoid such a job? White men's jobs pay more as a rule than jobs that members of other groups hold. Is it likely that blacks and women would not be attracted to a job for which white men, with all their access to other good jobs, can be recruited? If there are innocent reasons for workplace segregation, we have to conclude that the voluntary shunning by blacks and women of jobs historically held by white men is not one of them.

Maybe some blacks and white women would like a job in this restaurant, but their experience is exclusively in establishments that are less upscale. They might not be as qualified as the white men who are hired. The restaurant understandably favors those who have had experience in similar workplaces. After all, waiting on tables in such a restaurant requires such skills as deboning fish, recommending wine, explaining the various French or Italian dishes to customers in plain English, and so on. The need for that expertise might well lead to the hiring of experienced white men rather than inexperienced blacks and women, strictly on a merit basis. Is that the answer?

The "experience" and "qualifications" argument sounds plausible, but there is a big hole in it. If the only people ever hired to wait on tables in fancy restaurants are people who have experience in such restaurants, the corps of such waiters would inevitably shrink down to zero, as it was depleted by deaths, retirements, firings, and moves by waiters to other kinds of jobs. That does not happen, so we know that the corps of such waiters, like the corps of workers in any other occupation, is maintained by the recruitment of inexperienced people. Neophytes acquire the expertise required in such restaurants on the job. In fact, since the number of fancy restaurants is growing, the number of people entering the field as inexperienced recruits must be growing too.

To maintain an exclusively white male corps of waiters in fancy restaurants, all of the neophytes have to be white males. When an inexperienced candidate is hired, are the most promising candidates always inexperienced white males? Not just mostly white males but invariably and without exception white males? That is hard to believe, unless one also believes that there is something in blackness and femaleness that is always disqualifying.

The truth is that there is indeed something about blackness and femaleness that, while not formally disqualifying, leads in practice to the almost universal exclusion of those who are not white males from jobs as waiters in fancy restaurants. The problem is not that blacks and women lack the ability to learn the necessary skills on the job. Blacks and women are not hired to work in fancy restaurants because part of the "product" of such establishments is the projection of an ambiance like that in restaurants in Europe, where all the waiters are white males. (Similarly, in downtown Washington, D.C., there used to be a large restaurant that projected an "Old South" ambiance and hired only black male waiters. That would no longer be politically correct. In any case, the restaurant moved to the suburbs and now employs only white females to wait tables.) Blacks and females cannot project the traditional image of a "proper" waiter in a fancy restaurant. At least, they cannot project that image to the person doing the hiring.

The person who makes the hiring decisions in our hypothetical restaurant is concerned that customers, who are likely to expect a white man as their waiter, will think less of the restaurant if they are served by a different kind of waiter. The management may also attach some aesthetic value to the serving crew's uniformity by race and sex. The customers may be accustomed to gauging the fanciness of the restaurant and the legitimacy of its high prices at least in part by the race and gender of the waiters. The person making the hiring decisions has probably never asked any customers what they think about the race and gender of waiters, and how important it is to them to be served by a white man. The person doing the hiring may or may not be right about customers' reactions; right or wrong, however, his or her perception of what it takes to please customers is what determines the hiring outcome. That person may harbor no malice whatever toward minority people or women and in fact may generally favor a more equal society. Nevertheless, business is business.

The restaurant is in business to please its customers. Is it not legitimate and quite understandable that the restaurant would look for "merit" in job candidates that includes an ability to please

customers? Before answering yes to that question, we should consider the consequences.

If we endorse the idea that it is legitimate for the restaurant to
gratify the presumed expectation of its customers that they will be
waited on by white males, then we have endorsed a principle that
would lock many people out of many jobs. Under that principle, a
law firm or accounting firm could rule out black or female candidates for professional jobs because its clients might not respect or
trust them. We would have to allow the department store to refuse
to hire African American or Hispanic salespeople. (However, it
could hire them for the cleaning crew, where customers' expecta-
tions present no problem.) We would have to allow any firm to
consider white males only for executive positions if those in
charge of hiring believe that employees would not follow the leadership of anyone else.

If we say that employers, in making decisions about hiring, job
assignments, and promotions, can legitimately take into account
the belief of customers or of employees that only white males are
normal and appropriate in certain positions, we are then also saying that the present degree of job segregation by race and sex
should be allowed to go on indefinitely. After the Civil Rights Act
of 1964 was passed, employers who faced courtroom claims of discrimination because they had kept blacks and women out of certain jobs attempted to use customer tastes as a defense against the
charge. These employers claimed that their hiring decisions should

be allowed because they were based not on prejudice but on prudent business considerations. One case, decided in 1971, was similar to that of the fancy restaurant we have been discussing. The employer, a hotel that catered banquets and parties in its ballrooms, claimed that its business would be hurt if it hired waitresses because the customers expected and wanted male waiters.[1] In this and similar cases, the federal courts have ruled that people cannot be excluded from jobs because customers or fellow employees would be upset at their race or sex and the business would therefore be disadvantaged. Any employer who excludes prospective employees for such reasons is considered to be discriminating under the law.

(Most of the hotel dinners I go to are sponsored by feminist, civil rights, or scholarly organizations. The hotels must not be too concerned with pleasing since, despite the 1971 decision, almost all of the waiters who serve those dinners continue to be white males. The sponsoring organizations tend not to complain, and most of the diners do not even notice.)

In a case involving flight attendants, a federal appeals court said: "While we recognize that the public's expectation of finding one sex in a particular role may cause some initial difficulty, it would be totally anomalous if we were to allow the preferences and prejudices of the customers to determine whether the sex discrimination [practiced by an employer] was valid. Indeed, it was, to a large extent, these very prejudices the Act was meant to overcome."[2]

A restaurant that hires only white males as waiters has been

and is discriminating by race and sex within any reasonable interpretation of the law. How might it be moved to act differently? It
is unlikely to be sued by rejected applicants; most of them have
their living to make and consider their exclusion by such restaurants simply a fact of life. No government agency is likely to pay
much attention. The only likely source of pressure is the restaurant's
customers; in such a workplace, the evidence of discrimination is out
in the open for all of them to see. Some local antidiscrimination
groups have been effective in rousing customer sentiment against
restaurants that engage in segregated hiring practices. Some of these
restaurants have been moved to begin a bit of informal affirmative
action.

Discrimination is, of course, by no means confined to fancy
restaurants. There are many other jobs that do not require higher
education and for which only modest talents are needed; any special skills are learned on the job. Many such jobs pay relatively well
and are dominated by white men—over-the-road truck driving,
many construction jobs, lower-level administrative jobs, beginning
management jobs, or positions in car sales. Even pizza delivery
and valet parking are often dominated by white men.

Group Reputations

Human beings have a tendency to group other human beings, to
name those groups, and then to generalize about what their members
are like. We could never restrict ourselves to talking and thinking

only about individuals; group names and reputations are a way to organize the massive amounts of information we must deal with in our lives. We need to be able to talk about "my relatives," "women," "Republicans," "the elderly," "the Japanese." Inevitably, some of our generalizations about groups are going to be negative.

While grouping other human beings is necessary for organizing our thoughts, sensible and humane people understand that it carries a danger. They recognize the human tendency to overgeneralize about groups and to attribute to all members of a group the sins of some members. They know that some people think maliciously about certain groups, often for selfish or exploitative reasons; that some group reputations are undeserved. They know that even groups with deservedly bad reputations—teenagers, for example—have better and worse members; and that when dealing with individuals it is decent to reserve judgment. A bigot—and racism and sexism are, of course, modes of bigotry—is a person who is not sensible and decent in this way. It is not easy to avoid bigotry, and some people never try, including some of those with power over who gets hired or promoted.

The common generalizations about a certain group obviously influence the employment prospects of that group's members. Some researchers recently asked employers about their perceptions of blacks as job candidates. Not surprisingly, their study found that employers tend to have negative images of blacks as a group and to associate nonwhiteness with inferior education, lack of job skills, and unreliable job performance.[3]

The average black person is less skilled and less experienced than the average white, has been unemployed more often, had a rockier childhood, has fewer useful friends and contacts, and has gone to a lower-quality school. Yet hiring cannot be fair if employers take into account perceptions (even true ones) about the *average* black person when considering the individual black person applying to them for a job. Some individual black applicants are better than the average white candidate. To take all black applicants less seriously because black applicants on average are perceived to be a poor bet is bound to perpetuate the disadvantages suffered by black people. It may be rational behavior on the part of an employer, but it is unfair to individual black applicants and violates the law against discrimination.

The purpose of affirmative action is to help groups, that is, to help people who have been disadvantaged because of their group membership. Affirmative action programs oblige employers to consider the characteristics of individuals from previously excluded groups and to rely less on the reputations of those groups in judging the potential of individuals to do good work. Such programs, if they are to work, must force employers to confront the bigots in their organization and to cut off their power to exclude unfairly and to harass those they have failed to exclude.

Opponents of affirmative action argue that such programs reduce the focus on the merits of individuals because race and sex enter into hiring and promotion decisions. However, as we have seen, in most workplaces race and sex are taken into account whether affirmative action is being practiced or not. Without affirmative action, people of the "wrong" race or sex are too often dismissed automatically as serious candidates for certain jobs before their merits are ever considered.

Invisible Bias

In deciding which candidate should be hired, or which of two employees should be paid more, even well-meaning decision-makers may believe they are focusing only on merit while actually using biased methods. The psychologist Faye Crosby and her associates have done important experimental work that shows how this happens.[4]

Crosby created fictitious information about a supposed group of male and female managers, all working for the same fictitious company. Each manager's record showed his or her education, experience, efficiency rating, and current salary. An individual manager, male or female, might have a high score on some factors and a low score on others. Crosby made the males' and females' scores about equal on average in each of the three factors, so the overall merit ratings for the two sexes were equal on average. Crosby assigned the male managers considerably higher salaries on average than the female managers. The point of the experiment was to see whether people who looked at these made-up records could perceive that the company Crosby had created was systematically paying men more than women, despite the equal merit on average of the two sexes.

Crosby randomly assigned the people reviewing the records to two groups; both groups saw the same sets of records. The members of group 1 were shown the records in pairs, each pair consisting of a male manager's record and a female manager's record. After seeing a pair, members of group 1 were asked to judge whether the salaries of the man and the woman in the pair were aligned fairly. Then, after seeing all of the records and judging each pair, they were asked to make an overall judgment as to whether the company was fair to women managers. Those in group 2 saw the same records but were not asked to judge the fairness of salaries on a pair-by-pair basis. They were asked only to make an overall judgment of the company's fairness after seeing all the records.

One might have guessed that the members of group 1 would obtain a better understanding of the situation, but the opposite turned out to be true. Crosby found that more people in group 2 than in group 1 noticed that the company's pay practices were discriminatory. The reason was quite striking. By the time the members of group 1 had seen all the pairs, contemplated each set of salaries, and arrived at an overall judgment of the company, they had convinced themselves that in almost all of the pairs the male manager was more qualified than the female and deserved his higher salary. In each pair, the man was judged to deserve a higher salary than the woman if he was superior to her on any single one of the three factors used to measure about their relative merit. In other words, any factor that favored the man was given heavy weight, and any factor that favored the woman was ignored.

For example, if Mr. A, who was paired with Ms. B, had a lower efficiency rating and less education than she did, but more experience, his greater experience was considered the decisive proof that he merited a higher salary. In the next pair to be judged, Mr. C might have a higher efficiency rating than Ms. D, while she had more education and more experience; Mr. C's better efficiency rating was cited to show that he had greater merit than she. Experience, which was decisive for the man in the first case, was ignored in the second, where it favored the woman.

A series of decisions made in that way will result in the man being judged better than the woman in almost all cases. For a woman in a pair to be judged better, she has to be superior to the man she is being compared with on all counts, which would have happened in only one out of eight cases, if the two groups have equal merit.[5] Members of group 2 concentrated on trying to see what the pattern was from all of the evidence and were more able than the group 1 members to discern that the overall salary pattern was unduly favorable to the males.

Crosby's experiment is important for a number of reasons. First, it shows that people seem to want to believe, and are very ready to believe, that the better treatment of a member of a privileged group is justified by that person's merit. Any bit of evidence that might support that judgment is seized on and made decisive.

Any piece of evidence that contradicts it is likely to be ignored. Second, Crosby's experiment shows that people are more capable of judging whether a system is rigged in favor of one group over another when they review a collection of incidents together rather than one at a time.

This brings us back to affirmative action, and to real rather than fictional situations. In real life, most hirings and promotions happen one at a time, a condition under which, as Crosby's experiment shows, bias can easily creep in. Affirmative action asks questions like, "Are you going to appoint still another white person when the last ten appointed for this kind of job have been white?" It counteracts the tendency to look at each decision as an isolated event and puts new decisions in the context of all other recent decisions. Affirmative action can also lead to more formality and less subjectivity in judging candidates. In their eagerness to justify the favorable treatment of male managers, the group 1 members who reviewed Crosby's fictional records simply ignored evidence that interfered with making a judgment in favor of the male manager. Under a more formal process, the people judging candidates are more likely to be required to weigh all the evidence on all the candidates more consistently.

Crosby presented the people who reviewed her fictional records with just three items of information about each manager being judged. In real life, the number of factors can easily be expanded. If the African American candidate is better than the white one on all three factors originally presented, a fourth, fifth, or sixth factor may be introduced into the process until a factor on which the white candidate is superior can be found and made decisive. An experienced affirmative action officer can help everyone involved resist this tendency.

Lower Status Brings Harsher Treatment
in the Marketplace

Economists have theorized that treating people differently on account of their race or sex is generally a money-losing proposition. For that reason, most economists have believed that discrimination in the marketplace happens very rarely. Recent research has demonstrated that this is not true. When human beings engage in negotiations about money matters with people of low status they tend to drive harder bargains and treat them more harshly than they treat people of high status.

It has recently been shown that automobile dealers tend to offer markedly worse deals to women and African Americans than they offer to white men. As a result, the prices people in these groups pay for cars end up being significantly higher than those paid by white men. Originally, researchers felt that the higher prices might be due to the behavior of the buyers — they suspected that blacks and women might bargain less aggressively or less skillfully. So they took a diverse group of people, taught them all to bargain in the same style, and sent them out to visit car dealerships. The white men still ended up with better deals.[6]

In a striking experiment, another group of economists found that they could easily create artificial status differences that would affect the deals that people were offered. First they gave a roomful of students a five-question exam and took the papers outside the room to be graded. They came back with a list of students whom they said deserved gold stars as a result of their performance. Gold paper stars were awarded in a little ceremony, and displayed on the students' clothing for the rest of the session. (In actuality, the stars were given at random.) Then, students were paired off. One student in each pair was told to make a proposal to the other about how they would share a given sum of money. If the proposal was accepted, the money would be shared between the two students in the manner proposed; if it was rejected, neither student would get anything. The economists found that students without stars received proposals that were significantly worse on average than those with stars, whether those making the proposals had stars or not. The unstarred people receiving the proposals ended up with less money than those with the stars.[7]

The tendency to give harsh treatment to people of low status in economic transactions must surely affect outcomes in the job market. A vicious circle is set up—blacks' and women's bad results in the job market reinforces the impression that they have low status, which results in further poor treatment. Affirmative action can be seen as a way to break that vicious circle.

The Difficulty of Changing Hiring Habits

Patterns of occupational segregation by race and sex tend to persist in part because people have good reason to be cautious in making hiring and promotion decisions. These decisions are the most crucial to any organization's success. A bad mistake in hiring or promotion can result in large monetary losses and a lot of misery. When an unsuitable person has been chosen for a job, there may be painful weeks or months during which work is botched, tempers flare, feelings are bruised, and customers are alienated. Employers have an understandable tendency to move cautiously and to continue doing what has worked well previously. Hiring candidates of a different race or sex is likely to be seen as risky, as asking for trouble.

If a male candidate for a job held only by males in the past is highly acceptable, those in charge of making the selection may wonder why they should take a chance on a woman, even if she looks as though she could do the job. After all, a woman may not "work out." By the same token, if all previous successful incumbents in a certain job have been white and a white candidate who looks like a good bet is available, the natural tendency is not to take a chance on a black, not even on one who looks promising.

If the people involved in the selection process want to do nothing more than select the candidate who will perform the best, regardless of sex, race, or ethnicity, they are not likely to select a candidate of a nontraditional race or gender, even if very promising candidates of this kind are available. People use minimal clues of manner and appearance and way of talking to make snap judgments about candidates of a familiar type. A white person who has little experience with the performance of blacks on the job may not feel capable of making good judgments about their abilities based on such clues, and he or she may find it safer to stick with candidates of a familiar kind.

One way employers stick with the kinds of workers they are used to is by filling their vacancies with people recommended by those already working there in the kind of job they are filling. There is a considerable incentive for employers to fill jobs this way, and the practice is apparently widespread.[8] It saves recruiting expenses and may make for congenial work groups. A worker who recommends someone vouches for that person as someone likely to do well. Unfortunately, this seemingly innocent recruiting practice makes it particularly hard for African Americans to improve their status. Relying on employee recommendations effectively excludes from good jobs those who do not have relatives and friends with good jobs.

Women candidates may be particularly disadvantaged by sexual conventions. A woman who wears a standard amount of makeup and jewelry may be judged to be unbusinesslike, since the standard businessperson—a man—wears none. On the other hand, a woman who wears less than the standard amount of makeup and jewelry risks being considered not feminine enough to be a normal woman and is therefore judged to be peculiar. People making hiring decisions tend to shy away from people who seem peculiar.

Problems of Acceptance by Coworkers

Production on the job has its social aspects. Each worker has to learn from and teach others, engage in cooperative endeavors, transmit and receive information, help provide a friendly environment, cover occasionally for another's mistakes, and at least appear to be amused by the jokes that go around. The people doing the hiring customarily consider not only a candidate's technical abilities and general pleasantness but also the chances of the candidate being accepted by coworkers so that they will interact well.

Acceptance by coworkers may be problematical if the person hired is of atypical gender or race. When people who are not social equals are asked to interact on the job as equals, friction often develops. The way male construction workers typically interact with women may not be appropriate for a female colleague. Those who assign work to a male clerical worker may experience social discomfort ("Can I really ask a man to type 1,000 names and addresses for me? Won't it shame him?"). His presence may upset his female clerical coworkers as well ("Is he being bossy with me instead of a friend and an ally, like a woman would be?").

Some of the hostility to the worker of untraditional race or sex may be motivated by self-defense. Men know that jobs in which white males predominate tend to be compensated with high status and pay; feeling those benefits threatened, they may not welcome a coworker who dilutes the maleness or whiteness of their job.

They may fear that future vacancies will be filled with lower-status people or that they will have to leave the occupation or risk being trapped in a devalued job. As a result of such worries, there may be difficulties in convincing the old hands to introduce the newcomer of untraditional race or gender to the tricks of the trade.

Donald Tomaskovic-Devey reports an instance of this problem:

A pilot told me a story about the first woman pilot at the busy corporate airport where he worked. The other pilots knew from the start that she would not be able to cut it. To give her a "fair" chance to prove herself, they had decided not to show her the ropes, to allow her to figure out on her own the controls on planes she had not flown before, and not to introduce her to the control tower and maintenance staffs, although this information was routinely shared with new male pilots. After all, they knew from the start that a woman could not be a pilot. Of course, what they knew did not matter; it was what they did that was decisive. By refusing to share their knowledge, they insured her failure.[9]

The Need to Fix the Labor Market

We can summarize the discussion in this chapter and the previous one by saying that there is a great deal in the operation of the labor market that badly needs fixing—specifically, the persistent occupational segregation by race and sex, with the people on top mostly white and male. Most of the people making hiring and promotion decisions that perpetuate these patterns may not be consciously malicious. But many people do think stereotypically—imputing low abilities to all blacks, for instance—and many have strong beliefs about women's proper place. Many people do not give issues of sex or race much thought. They believe that they already behave fairly, and that they are filling vacancies with the best people available.

Because most people believe in their own rectitude, we cannot expect a great deal of progress in integrating the workplace by race and by sex without a systematic program that pushes people to act differently. The purpose of affirmative action is to supply that push.

four

Goals: Splitting the Pie

In some parts of the world, when a pie is to be shared by family members, the men and boys are served first. After they have eaten their fill, the women and girls get whatever is left, if anything. In the West, by contrast, the norm is for the males and females in the family to be served together, and for each family member to have an approximately equal share of the pie. The individual slices may vary somewhat according to who is hungriest or who particularly likes the pie being served. Nevertheless, it is assumed that some of the pie is reserved for the females and some for the males of the family proportional to their respective numbers. The server divides up the pie keeping in mind that neither group should be systematically shortchanged.

In the West, we abolished the tradition of male privilege in the portioning out of food and other goods and services within the family long ago. Male privilege has just begun to be challenged in employment, however, and it is not yet abolished. We have only recently challenged the privilege of whites in employment. In many lines of work, white males have been and continue to be served as much pie as they want, as we have seen in the last two chapters.[1] Drawing up goals for an affirmative action plan is the equivalent of saying that we want to end the tradition of giving white males as much pie as they want at the expense of all other groups.

Affirmative action is based on the belief that the groups who have been monopolizing the best jobs are not the only ones suited to them. The goals in an affirmative action plan should represent a careful and unbiased view of what kinds of people can be expected to do which jobs competently. Affirmative action goals are not necessarily proportional to group size. They need to reflect the availability of qualified people for each kind of job in each group. Nevertheless, setting affirmative action goals and sharing the family pie have this in common: they are both done in the understanding that historic privileges are unfair, and should not persist.

Goals as Energizing Devices

When critics of affirmative action say that goals are the same as quotas, and that quotas are bad, they presumably are saying, "Get rid of discrimination if there is any; give everyone a fair chance.

But make sure you don't measure success or failure in numbers. If you do, you may be tempted to do some unfair and stupid things to make the numbers look good." The problem is that the directive "Be fair from now on" is far less energizing, and far more easily evaded, than "There are some good black people out there. Have one of them aboard by a month from next Thursday, or at least show that you've tried." Recruitment methods are highly resistant to change. And as our review of labor market realities has shown, there are many workplaces where these methods need changing if we are to make significant progress toward fairness.

The use of numerical goals to spur managers into action and to direct their behavior has been useful in all aspects of modern management; indeed, its use in affirmative action follows from its success in other areas. Modern businesses use numerical goals to manage production, productivity, sales, investments, and costs. The announcement of goals helps to specify explicit standards for performance of managers. In the absence of numerical goals and timetables for meeting them, it is difficult to determine whether managers have done a good job or to hold anyone responsible for failures. When people know they will not be held responsible, they are less likely to make significant efforts.

Goals are particularly important when what needs to be accomplished is difficult and possibly distasteful to those who have to bring it about. In affirmative action, managers are asked to do things that are unfamiliar, that may seem to them risky in terms of productivity, and that are very possibly distasteful to them personally.

Ending segregation in a work group by hiring the first woman or the first black often takes courage. Managers have to face the resistance that may arise from their peers, from the employees they supervise, or from their customers. They may have to overcome their own biases. In the absence of goals and a system of rewards for meeting goals, it is natural for managers to let such difficult matters slide, putting them off indefinitely.

If a sizable number of hires or promotions are going to be made all at once, progress in combating discrimination may be made even without formal goals just on the strength of repeated exhortations to fairness and diversity. Such exhortations might lead people to think, "We are going to announce twenty promotions next month. These days it won't look so good if they are all white males. Maybe the group should have some blacks and some women in it."

Goals, and their enforcement, are far more necessary in the more common situation: hirings and promotions that are done one at a time. When a single decision is made, the cost of raising a fuss about hiring still another white male is high. The cost of letting one more opportunity to make progress slip by is viewed as small or nonexistent. Moreover, the white or male candidate chosen is sure to be better in at least one job qualification than the black or female candidate not chosen. As we have seen from the work of Faye Crosby and her associates, that fact provides a handy rationale for hiring one white male after another.

Having goals and timetables in a plan that stays in somebody's file cabinet is not sufficient. Traditional patterns of segregation yield only if managers up and down the organization—all of those in a position to influence the hiring and promotion process— understand that a judgment of how well they have performed in furthering the integration of the workplace will be an important ingredient in the evaluation of their own job performance, and that the success of their own career with the organization will be affected. Managers have preconceptions and habits that inhibit change. In the absence of rewards and punishments, they cannot be expected to pursue desegregation vigorously. Indeed, affirmative action plans that lack implicit or explicit rewards and punishments for those with the power to hire and promote are usually dead letters.

How Are Goals Like Quotas? Are Quotas Always Bad?

The opponents of affirmative action insist that the goals of affirmative action plans constitute quotas. Making this association is an attempt to discredit goals by putting them in the same category as the quotas against Jewish students that elite colleges maintained prior to 1945. There are certainly some similarities between the quota on Jewish students and the goals of affirmative action. In both cases, people's membership in a group is noticed and allowed to influence what happens to them. Quotas limited Jewish students to a certain share of places; affirmative action goals also limit white males to a certain share of hires or promotions.

However, there are important differences. Jews were treated as unworthy of full participation in society, and the quotas were part of that treatment. White males are often treated as the only ones fully worthy; affirmative action goals are a way to chip away at their excess of privilege. At the time of the Jewish quotas, it was common for Jews to be discriminated against in what jobs they could hold and in where they could live. The Jewish quotas restricted members of a relatively disfavored group; affirmative action goals restrict members of the groups that are most favored in our society: whites, men, and particularly white men. The Jewish quotas reserved valuable societal resources for the "haves." The purpose of affirmative action goals is to pry away a fraction of the resources for the "have-nots," resources they have been denied on account of discrimination. No one pretended that a larger and beneficial social purpose was served by the anti-Jewish quotas—except, perhaps, the purpose of sparing non-Jews the presence and competition of too many Jews. The Jewish quotas kept an out group out. Affirmative action goals are intended to end the exclusion of out groups.

Goals and the Principle of Nondiscrimination

The Civil Rights Act of 1964 declares it unlawful to "deprive any individual of employment opportunities or otherwise adversely affect his status as an employee, because of such individual's race, color, religion, sex, or national origin."[2] When the bill was being debated, Sen. Hubert Humphrey, one of the chief sponsors of the legislation, was asked whether the bill would countenance quotas, and he said that it would not.[3]

Goals or quotas can lead to "reverse discrimination": refusing to consider certain people for a job or promotion on the grounds that their appointment to the next slot would thwart the achievement of a goal because they are white or male. The male who might have been appointed attorney general had President Bill Clinton not wanted three women in the cabinet was a "victim" of a goal. It is certainly not far-fetched to argue that the Civil Rights Act should be read as forbidding goals set with regard to representation by race or sex, on the grounds that they inevitably cause violations of the Act's prohibition on adversely affecting anyone's status on account of race or sex. Nevertheless, the Supreme Court has allowed employers to use race-based and sex-based remedies that favor blacks and women in their efforts to end occupational segregation in their workplaces. Goals have been allowed without a legal finding that segregation in a workplace was the result of past discrimination on the part of the employer.

In *Steelworkers v. Weber*, the Court said it was legal for the Kaiser Steel Company to set up a training program in which half the slots were reserved for minority workers in order to correct the exclusion of blacks from the ranks of its skilled workers.[4] In *Johnson v. Transportation Agency*, the Court allowed a woman to be promoted in accordance with an affirmative action plan to desegregate all-male jobs.[5] Her promotion superseded the regular promotion procedure, which had resulted in the choice of a male for the job. An interpretation of the Civil Rights Act that allows goals by race and sex has two important elements: an awareness of the situation the Act was intended to correct, and a view of what is necessary to correct that situation.

The racial discrimination to which the Civil Rights Act responded was not an offense (like driving while drunk) that a white or black might have committed, that had caused injury both to blacks and whites, and that needed to be controlled as much for the benefit of one group as another. Rather, the country, and particularly the South, had been in the grip of a caste system, and blacks were the subordinate caste. All the injuries and insults of racial discrimination had been suffered by them. The Act's primary purposes were to end segregation, to usher black people into full participation in the nation's economic life as employees and customers, and to ensure them the status of first-class citizens.[6] The Act's endorsement of the principle of nondiscrimination in employment can be seen as providing a means to those particular ends.

As to the means for ending the caste system, a majority on the Supreme Court believed that race-conscious actions by employers would be necessary. This belief was not based on philosophy or ethics, nor was it based on a systematic examination of case studies or on the results of controlled experiments designed to show what works and what does not. Rather, it was a commonsense judgment of what is possible in the world we live in. This judgment must have been shared by a majority of the Court at the time the *Weber* and *Johnson* cases were decided.

The rationale for *Weber* and *Johnson* can be made clearer by drawing an analogy with the antidiscrimination aims of the Americans with Disabilities Act of 1990. Significant progress in providing appropriate employment opportunities for disabled people will be made only if employers actively look for jobs in their workplaces that they might perform and actively look for disabled individuals to fill them. Numerical goals for the disabled would systematize and energize such efforts. But marking off slots for them would undoubtedly result in some nondisabled people being turned down for some jobs. Some might call those nondisabled people "victims of reverse discrimination." Should the Americans with Disabilities Act be construed or amended to forbid such "reverse discrimination"? To answer affirmatively, one would have to believe the absurd: that a major purpose of that act is or should be the protection of the able-bodied from discrimination that might be inflicted upon them on account of their nondisabled condition.

The idea that significant progress could be made in reducing the exclusion of the disabled with a "disabilities-blind" approach is manifestly ludicrous. People cannot blind themselves to a candidate's state of disability. The idea that we could break the pattern of sex and race segregation by ordering people doing the hiring to be sex-blind or race-blind is no less ludicrous. Only after desegregation takes place and it has become a commonplace that

African Americans, white women, and the disabled perform competently in many jobs from which they are now absent will we be able to begin ignoring sex, race, and disability in making employment decisions.

Some legal scholars, both liberal and conservative, have disagreed with the tenor of Supreme Court decisions as represented in *Weber* and *Johnson*; they have argued that the Civil Rights Act should be construed as forbidding any activity or procedure that requires taking account of the race and sex of individuals in deciding how to treat them. They also believe that the equal protection requirement imposed by the Constitution, properly interpreted, outlaws government affirmative action programs. Supreme Court Justices Antonin Scalia and Clarence Thomas are of this opinion. They and three other justices joined in 1995 in a five-to-four decision in *Adarand Constructors, Inc. v. Peña* to require that government affirmative action programs be based only on the government's "compelling interest," subject to "strict scrutiny" for constitutionality, and that they be "narrowly tailored" to remedy the effects of specifically documented discrimination.[7] *Adarand* does not outlaw all affirmative action, as Justices Scalia and Thomas would like. However, if this conservative group on the Court continues to prevail, affirmative action programs will become more difficult to sustain legally, just as they are becoming more difficult to sustain politically.

Employers may legally set goals for any group not covered by the Civil Rights Act. If the views of Scalia and Thomas were to prevail, the only way to legalize employers' systematic programs to rectify the exclusion of women and blacks from jobs would be for Congress to remove from the Act the protection against job discrimination for reasons of race and sex—a paradoxical situation indeed.

In a dissent in the *Adarand* case, Justice John Paul Stevens said:

The consistency [in forbidding government use of race in both "prejudicial" and "benign" ways] that the Court espoused would disregard the difference between a "No Trespassing" sign and a welcome mat. . . . It would equate a law that made black citizens ineligible for military service with a program aimed at recruiting black soldiers. An attempt by the majority to exclude members of a minority race from a regulated market is fundamentally different from a subsidy that enables a relatively small group of newcomers to enter that market. An interest in "consistency" does not justify treating differences as though they were similarities.[8]

Goals for Whom?

One of the most controversial aspects of goals is deciding who is to be specified in them. Beyond separate goals for white women, black women, and black men, for what other groups should there be goals? Should there also be goals for male and female Hispanics? Male and female people of Japanese, Hungarian, or Irish extraction? How about Catholics and Mormons? Should there be goals for disabled people? For the aged? If we have any detailed goals at all, is there a reasonable stopping point in the subdivision of the job pie?

If we were to establish goals for both sexes and for each of the ethnic groups represented in the United States, the labor market would become a balkanized nightmare: each slot would be earmarked for a person of a particular extraction and gender. Moreover, an expansion of the share of the population for whom goals are set might have an adverse impact on groups for which no goals are set, groups that contain relatively large numbers of high achievers—Jews and Asians, for example. A severe shrinking of the proportion of the population not included in affirmative action goals might reduce tolerance of the high success rates of such groups. In short, there are good reasons to have fewer goals rather than more. Establishing goals for a particular group should not be done without substantial reason. There is no sign that we are tending in the direction of an overproliferation of groups covered by affirmative action goals.

Common sense suggests that employment goals should be set for a group only if all of the following conditions are met:

1) The group is seriously underrepresented in an occupation or at a hierarchical level in the workplace.
2) The underrepresentation continues because of present discrimination, or because of current employer practices or habits that effectively exclude members of the group.

3) The pattern of exclusion is unlikely to change in the absence of special efforts.

For jobs in which discriminated-against groups are overrepresented, goals should be set for integrating whites and males into them. This effort will fail if the salaries for such jobs are significantly lower than what white males with the required skills can earn in other jobs. Nor will it be possible to recruit white males into jobs that have obviously been set up as dead ends, jobs whose duties are overly repetitive, or jobs over which the supervision is more rigid than white males of that skill level are used to. Integrating the all-female jobs with males, or the all-black jobs with whites, will force employers to rethink wage levels and working conditions—to the benefit of those members of disadvantaged groups who stay in traditionally sex- or race-specific occupations.

Different areas of the country, occupations, industries, and hierarchical levels call for different sets of goals. The evidence suggests that goals are needed almost everywhere for black men and women and white women, and in many places for Hispanics of both sexes. The Civil Rights Act would forbid discrimination against people of Hungarian extraction on account of their origin. However, if there is no reason to think that Hungarians are being excluded, we should not have goals for them.

Consider, however, the situation of a New England law firm that employs forty lawyers and has no partners or associates of Irish or Jewish extraction. There are many people of Irish extraction in

New England, and a considerable number of Jews as well. In the past these groups were commonly denied access to jobs reserved for upper-crust males of British extraction. Many lawyers of Irish and Jewish extraction now have elite legal credentials, and if a firm of that size has no such lawyers on its staff, it is likely that some aspects of the recruitment process are keeping them from being hired. Our guidelines suggest that having a goal for hiring lawyers of Irish and Jewish ancestry would be desirable for this firm. On the other hand, in other parts of the country, and in some occupations in which being of Irish or Jewish ancestry has not recently been a substantial disadvantage, goals for such people, even when they are underrepresented, would be unnecessary and undesirable.

Goals for disabled people in each sizable workplace would be very much in the national interest. We tend to shun the disabled, according to the sociologist Irving Goffman, because we lack a familiar "script" for interacting with them.[9] Disabled people are often excluded from work they could perform well largely because of the social unease their presence might cause. To the difficulties caused by their disability are added the burdens of their unnecessarily narrowed work opportunities. The passage of the Americans with Disabilities Act made discrimination against disabled people illegal; adding goals for them to affirmative action plans would translate the Act's good intentions into a more substantial reality.

What about goals for gays and lesbians? There is some evidence that, after education and experience are accounted for, people who tell survey researchers they are homosexual are moderately less successful in the job market than heterosexuals.[10] Homosexuals appear to be "coming out of the closet" in greater numbers. Whether their greater visibility will make for increased tolerance or increased discrimination remains to be seen. Nevertheless, unless more serious discrimination against them than is known to exist can be shown, the case for employment goals for gays and lesbians is not strong.[11]

Discontinuing Goals

Affirmative action goals are not meant to last forever. Goals for a group should be discarded when its members have become well integrated into the labor market—that is, when there is a good flow of candidates, when discriminatory attitudes have waned, when there is no prejudice against hiring members of that group, and when the group has for some time been represented in the workforce at appropriate levels in a full range of occupations. We no longer have a "Jewish seat" on the Supreme Court because it is no longer needed as a way to ensure the access of Jews to appointment to the Court. We still need black and female seats on the Court. But we can certainly look forward to the time when we will not need them, and when goals for blacks and women as police officers, carpenters, or bond salespeople will be unnecessary as well.[12]

five

Thinking about Fairness

Imagine yourself as a white man, waiting in line on a street corner for the next bus, in the rain, with other white men. You are nervous, because the line is long and there probably won't be room on the next bus for everyone waiting. The buses seem to be coming less frequently lately. A black man comes to the corner, accompanied by a police officer. The officer says that the black man is going to get on the next bus and he, the officer, is here to see that he does. That's unfair, you say. Why doesn't he get in line like the rest of us? Why should preference be given to him?

The black man says that he has tried getting in line like everybody else. But when buses stop to take on passengers at this corner, the drivers, who have some discretion as to who is allowed to board, may say to a black person in line, "You don't look quite right to me. I'm not letting you on." Sometimes there are arguments about the order in which people arrived at the corner. The facts are unclear, and the blacks lose those arguments. The result is that very few blacks have managed to board a bus on this particular route. In fact, blacks don't even bother to wait for this bus anymore. The police officer is here to see that things change, starting now.

The white people at the bus stop point out that they are not the ones who have kept blacks off the bus, if that ever really happened. Let's remember, they say, that this black man would take the place on the bus of a white man who has been following the rules of the bus stop and patiently waiting in the rain. That white man shouldn't have to give up his place just because he's white. He may have had a rougher life than this black man who is being given special treatment. The officer should go away and let the black man be treated just like everybody else. We whites have our rights too; stop victimizing us.

At that point, the bus rolls up. We can see through the windows that the only people on board are whites. Ah, says the black man, what do you think would happen if the policeman were to go away right now?

Difficult Issues

The parable of the bus stop brings up two of the most difficult issues that proponents of affirmative action have to face if they are to convince people that affirmative action on balance serves justice.

The first is, of course, fairness to the individual displaced: the white man who will be left out in the rain. The second is the violation of a procedure that looks fair.

The bus stop parable also introduces some of the issues that the opponents of affirmative action need to face. The most important is the raw fact of the persistence of segregation: the buses that come by on the particular route at issue have no black people on them. Another problem for the opponents is the fairness in actuality of a selection system that looks fair in theory. A third issue is the degree of harm done to the displaced individual, and whether avoiding any harm whatever to that individual should outweigh all other considerations. A fourth issue facing the opponents of affirmative action is that the method of ending segregation they espouse has not worked.

Merit and Diversity

Achieving diversity—ending segregation—and picking the best qualified candidate for a job are not necessarily inconsistent. Well-administered affirmative action programs seek out qualified women and blacks and remove barriers to their proper consideration. Under affirmative action, some black candidates will be more promising than their white rivals; some women will be more promising than their male rivals. In situations where there has been discrimination, removing it can promote both diversity and merit. In the absence of affirmative action more promising blacks may lose out to less promising whites.

We do not know what degree of diversity could be achieved without infringing on selection by perceived merit. The evidence on segregation by sex and race shows widespread ongoing discrimination, much of it in the placement of newly hired people in particular jobs. As we have seen, in many workplaces newly hired blacks are automatically placed in "black jobs," and women in "women's jobs." Much segregation could be abolished by bringing in a more diverse group of candidates, reforming the assignment process, and ending any bias in assessing merit. Desegregating training programs such as apprenticeships can create good black and female candidates.

Sometimes, however, no black or female candidate for a particular slot in a segregated line of work will emerge who seems as promising to those doing the judging as the white or male candidates available. The foes of affirmative action take their stand on such cases, insisting that choosing the blacks or females who are qualified, but are not top-ranked, for the purpose of ending segregation is always wrong. They argue that we must without exception use merit as the only criterion for selection. This position is powerfully appealing. We would all like to be treated with respect and to have our virtues given due weight. It is painful to think that one's career and happiness might be damaged by a social engineering scheme.

Nevertheless, an individual's pain, or the harm done to that individual, is not all that is at stake. What is also at stake is the desirability of ending segregation. The question is whether the former should ever be traded off for the latter. The opponents of affirmative action imply by their arguments that causing harm to innocent individuals so as to achieve some other benefit is totally impermissible and never done, but that is not true. In our economic life, we frequently do harm to innocent individuals for the purpose of achieving some goal. Keeping the unemployment rate high to fight off inflation is one example. That does substantial harm to millions of people. Another is firing workers so that a company can reduce its costs.

In considering the possible tradeoff of harm to an individual for the benefits of diversity—making the offer to the second-ranked or the sixth-ranked candidate, or even on occasion the twenty-sixth— we first have to consider two issues: whether measurements of merit always establish who is truly best, and what, if any, value should be placed on diversity in a workplace—on ending segregation by race or sex. After that discussion, we will be in a better position to judge whether merit should ever be traded off for diversity.

The Fuzziness of Merit

We frequently think and act as though there were only one correct way to define merit, one right and infallibly accurate way to measure it, and one right way to use measurements of merit in making hiring or school admission decisions. We also tend to assume that these obviously right ways are everywhere in current use. They are not, of course.

The rankings of candidates as to merit will depend on which of the candidates' characteristics are taken into consideration, how much weight is given to each characteristic, and how the judging is done—formally, objectively, and consistently for all candidates, or informally and inconsistently. Faye Crosby's research, described in chapter 3, shows that people do unconsciously give more weight to the good points of the person they consider appropriate for the job (for instance, a white man for a management job) and tend to ignore the good points of a person they think is less appropriate.

In thinking about affirmative action erroneous assumptions are frequently made:

1) That for each job opening there is one person who is unambiguously the best among the candidates.

2) That the identity of that candidate is unerringly revealed by the employer's selection process.

3) That the evaluation process is uninfluenced by the sex, race, ethnicity, age, or disability status of the candidates.

4) That the "best" candidate is head and shoulders above all the others, so that the substitution of the one judged third- or fourth-best instead of the one judged best would make a great difference to productivity.

These assumptions are unrealistic in many, even most cases. The American Society for Personnel Administration, in a brief supporting affirmative action in a case before the Supreme Court, said:

> It is a standard tenet of personnel administration that there is rarely a single, "best qualified" person for a job. An effective personnel system will bring before the selecting official several fully-qualified candidates who each may possess different attributes which recommend them for selection. Especially where the job is an unexceptional, middle-level craft position, without the need for unique work experience or educational attainment and for which several well-qualified candidates are available, final determinations as to which candidate is "best qualified" are at best subjective.[1]

The selection process often does have important subjective elements, allowing plenty of leeway for making mistakes as well as for decision-makers' attitudes about race and gender to influence outcomes. Thus, it is wrong to assume that the candidate chosen in the absence of affirmative action is always or almost always better than all of those sent away. It is wrong to assume that a woman or a minority male not crowned with the judgment of "best" but nevertheless judged to be quite adequate will, when placed in a job under an affirmative action plan, perform worse than the person who might otherwise have been selected.

Measurements of merit for a job or for school admission, then, are dependent on the methods used and subject to error and subversion; moreover, they may not differentiate among candidates with any great accuracy. A process of assessing merit that cuts out all but white males may mask purposeful discrimination or set up hurdles that female and black candidates, for no job-related reason, have particular difficulty in getting over. An interviewer whose method of measuring congeniality is to chat with candidates about golf is not going to be giving very many black or female candidates high grades for that quality.

If we have a way of measuring merit that has been used in the past, is it fair to make changes that will improve the ratings of black and women candidates? The established procedure may not be maximally fair and efficient. If the established method has eliminated most women or most black people, conscious or unconscious bias is certainly a possible reason.

A foe of affirmative action might respond, "Certainly if the method of judging merit has flaws, then by all means change it. All I ask is that it not be changed for the sole purpose of increasing the representation of the previously excluded groups." By this reasoning, it would be legitimate to change the method of judging merit to reduce the employer's cost of making selections among candidates, or to shorten the time the selections consume, or to make the process more convenient for those doing the judging, but it would not be legitimate to change it for the purpose of ending race or sex segregation. In practice, institutions, firms, and individuals do make changes in the way they judge merit for the purpose of reducing cost and inconvenience. Such changes are not generally deemed unfair to the people who would have been winners under the old system but are losers in the new one.

The Benefits of Diversity

I have already noted the benefits of diversity in the president's cabinet and in police forces that serve racially diverse populations. Diversity prevents power from being concentrated in any one group and promises sympathetic and fair treatment to all sections of the public. Besides government officials and police officers, other examples of occupations in which diversity is especially important include journalists and others working in media, physicians, social workers, models in mail-order catalogs, judges (and therefore lawyers), managers and other people in authority, and politicians and other government employees. One of the major benefits of diversity is that it makes visible an organization's adherence to the principle that no type of person is excluded from performing any function, including responsible, important, and prestigious ones.

Another benefit of diversity is the differing points of view, insights, values, and knowledge of the world that members of various groups bring to their roles. Examples of the harmfulness of lack of diversity are easy to find. In the United States, medical researchers have repeatedly studied large groups of subjects consisting entirely of males and done no corresponding studies on groups of female subjects. The result has been that we know a lot more about men's health than about women's. Women in Congress and women medical researchers, newly increased in numbers and power, have lately challenged that practice. In decades of research on poverty, the economics profession, dominated by white males, ignored the concentration of poverty among female single parents and the problems they faced with sex discrimination in the labor market, with child care costs, and with child support enforcement. Researchers also largely ignored racial discrimination as a leading cause of poverty.

Diversity is especially important in some situations, but it might be argued that in a racially diverse society there is some positive value to having diversity in any sizable work group, regardless of its function. Leading a segregated life on the job makes workers less fit for life in a community where respect for all groups is supposed to be the rule. All-male crews sometimes aggravate the misogyny of those who serve in them, and all-white crews sometimes aggravate racism. In all-male and all-white groups, disparaging remarks about those not represented are likely to be uncontradicted, and attitudes harden.

Perhaps the most important reason for valuing the introduction of diversity into workplaces is that it helps dismantle two caste systems—one based on race and another based on gender—that have been responsible for a great deal of misery. A caste system dictates that your social status forever be that which you were born into, limits your choice of occupations, regardless of your talents and taste, and visits automatic disrespect on those at the bottom of the caste pecking order. The fate of many of those at the bottom of the race caste system is poverty. The fate of many of those at the bottom of the sex caste system is a choice between poverty and dependency. Our caste systems based on race and sex were in full flower until quite recently, and the remnants of them are still very much with us.

Passing over the "Most Qualified"

When, if ever, is it ethically right to pass over the person judged "most qualified" and to take instead a person judged to be less qualified who will add diversity? Some might argue that diversity should never be given priority on the grounds that it has no value and therefore nothing good should be traded off for it. Alternatively, one might argue that race and sex should never affect the way people are treated, so that we must be blind to diversity's presence or absence. One might take the position that considering only merit is so ethically important that it cannot be traded off for any other consideration, such as diversity, even if diversity were judged to have value. These arguments, especially the last one, do not accord with common American thinking and practice.

If it were generally agreed that it is ethically important never to consider anything but merit (in the technical sense of the predicted ability to perform the major function for which the person is being selected), then we would not have veterans' preferences, or the preferential admissions of the children of alumni to Harvard. Or at least, there would be protests against these practices. They are tolerated, however, and never protested; therefore the unfairness of considering only merit cannot be a principle that is universally recognized and considered important. As a general principle, nobody seems to care very much. Only its application to race seems to resonate.

Those who advocate not paying attention to race and sex as an inviolable principle would enshrine something that is impossible under present labor market conditions unless employers start hiring people without interviews. The degree of segregation that exists in the labor market shows that sex and race are indeed noticed—to the detriment of women and blacks—when most hiring and placement decisions are made. The idea that we could, starting next week, make people switch off their perception of a person's race and sex and switch off their ideas about who belongs in which job is ludicrous. The people in a segregated workplace who have been noticing sex and race to the detriment of blacks and women will go right on doing so unless a program is installed that will notice the race and sex of applicants for jobs and schools for the purpose of dismantling the system of segregation.

Some of the foes of affirmative action have revealed their attitudes on whether the achievement of diversity is worthwhile in their reactions to a case in Piscataway, New Jersey.[2] A school there had to lay off a teacher, and the choice was between a white woman and a black woman. They judged the two as having identical qualifications. The school opted to keep the black teacher because she was the only black in the business education department. The white teacher brought suit on the grounds that her firing was a case of "reverse discrimination"—she was fired because of her race. The Justice Department under President Bush, dominated by foes of affirmative action, submitted court briefs supporting the white teacher's side of the case. In doing so, the Bush administration implicitly assigned a zero value to diversity.

It is illuminating to think about other ways by which the tie in merit between the Piscataway teachers might have been broken. The school administrators might have looked at aspects of merit not yet taken into account. For example, they could have counted the number of sick days the two teachers had taken: this method of breaking the tie would have given the students the benefit of retaining the teacher who, based on past performance, was a bit more likely to show up in class every day. They might have given the teachers a speech test, and had the benefit of retaining the one best fitted to be a good English-language model for the students. The "fair" solution that would probably occur to most people would be to flip a coin. This, however, would have provided the school and the students with no apparent benefit.

The school administrators chose instead to retain the teacher whose presence would convey to the students that both blacks and whites were fit to teach business education, and to continue to provide the black students with something the white business education students would retain—a role model of their own race they could identify with. It is possible also that the effect of retaining the black teacher on the social and economic health of the historically underprivileged black community, and therefore on the civic health of the community as a whole, was considered in making the decision. If these factors were considered, can we say that taking them into account was ethically less sound than flipping a coin or counting the sick days?

Was an injustice done to the white teacher because her race was taken into account, and used against her? If she had lost out because of one extra sick day, or because her pronunciation was slightly less standard than that of the other teacher, one might say that her interests were sacrificed to a legitimate purpose of the school, although a relatively minor one. In actuality, her interests were sacrificed to another purpose of the school — that the school might have the benefit of maintaining racial diversity — and perhaps to the community's interest in greater equality between black and white citizens. Is the sacrifice of her interests less ethically sound in one case than in the other?

Of course, taking fewer sick days or speaking better standard English come under the heading of personal merit, while contributing to racial diversity and raising the average income and status in the black community arguably do not. (Winning a coin flip would not testify to personal merit, either.) The case of the Piscataway teachers suggests that factors besides those testifying to personal merit can ethically enter into the decision.

We have too easily fallen into the habit of thinking that firms, institutions, and schools exist to provide playing fields where people come to have their narrowly defined merit tested by certain fixed and immutable procedures. But they are not tennis stadiums whose sole purpose is to provide arenas for tests of skill, where the trophy must be awarded to the one who has won the most sets in the match played that day. Therefore, the contestants have no right to expect that any particular procedure for deciding who is selected will be followed. Employers, institutions, and schools have other worthy purposes. Not every purpose for which a school or an employer puts aside measures of merit is worthy, but some of them are. Fulfilling such worthy purposes does not necessarily make their dealings with individuals unethical. Ending an unethical regime of segregation that has favored historically privileged groups, or avoiding resegregation as in the Piscataway case, should count among such worthy purposes.

The argument that measurements of merit are all that should ever count rests on very weak foundations. Attention should be paid to the importance of both merit and diversity. The reader may consider the ethical question in the context of the following case, in which diversity was valued over merit (or perhaps "merit").

Merit Versus Diversity: An Example

The records of court cases allow us to observe what goes on in segregated workplaces, some of the devices used to keep them segregated, and how affirmative action might work, before sizing up the fairness of the results. The facts of a case that went to the Supreme Court illustrates well some on-the-job realities. Diane Joyce had been working for four years as an account clerk at the Santa Clara County Transportation Agency, whose mission is to maintain county roads. When a higher-paying position as a road dispatcher opened up, Joyce applied for it.[3] Dispatchers assign road crews, equipment, and materials and maintain records on the road maintenance work to be done. The dispatcher job was one of 238 positions in the agency classified as "skilled crafts worker." Not a single one of those positions had ever been held by a woman. The Santa Clara County Transportation Agency had an affirmative action plan, but up to that point not much had been done to deseg-regate a workplace that was highly segregated by sex.

Joyce was told that she was ineligible for the dispatcher posi-tion because she had not served as a road maintenance worker. There were 110 road maintenance jobs in the agency, and none of them had ever been held by a woman either. Joyce was allowed to take a job in the road maintenance crew, but her experience there was not easy. Her first supervisor was apparently not inclined to welcome her. Male workers were routinely provided with coveralls to protect their clothing, but none were given to her. After ruining one set of clothes, she complained to the supervisor, but nothing was done. After her clothing was ruined three more times, she filed a formal grievance. The next day, before the grievance could be formally processed, Joyce was issued the four pairs of coveralls that the men were routinely given.

Joyce worked on road maintenance crews for almost five years and during that period filled in temporarily as a road dispatcher on a number of occasions. She also served as chair of the Roads Operations Safety Committee. When a regular job as a road dispatcher again opened up, she applied for it. Joyce was one of nine applicants for the position who were deemed "well qualified." Another applicant was a man named Paul Johnson; his career with the agency had been similar to Diane Joyce's. He had joined the agency three years before Joyce did and had had some previous dispatcher experience, although he had worked only two years on road maintenance crews, compared with her five years.

The candidates were called to an interview with a two-person board. The board gave the candidates numerical scores, all of them between 70 and 80. Paul Johnson was tied for second with a 75, while Diane Joyce was next with a score of 73. The last and decisive interview was with a three-person board of agency supervisors. One of the members of that board was the supervisor who had behaved antagonistically toward Joyce when she joined the road maintenance crew and against whom she had been forced to file a grievance. A second was a man with whom she had had a disagreement in her capacity as chair of the safety committee. He had called her a "rebel-rousing [sic], skirt-wearing person." The three supervisors recommended that Paul Johnson be promoted to the dispatcher's job.

Diane Joyce sought the help of the agency's affirmative action officer. He recommended to the top management that the job go to her, and she was placed in the job. Paul Johnson sued the agency, charging that he had been kept out of the job on account of his sex, and that what had occurred should be viewed as sex discrimination. The case eventually reached the Supreme Court. The Court upheld the agency in placing Joyce instead of Johnson in the job.

The case illustrates the difficulties in breaking down occupational segregation even in a public agency with an affirmative action plan. It also exemplifies the merit issue: in all likelihood, the assessment of merit in this case produced fuzzy results.

In his dissenting opinion, Justice Antonin Scalia argued ardently that Johnson was treated unfairly. Scalia portrayed Johnson as an underdog victim of sex discrimination. In addition, he argued that relatively unskilled people like Johnson are

> members of the nonfavored groups *least* likely to have profited
> from societal discrimination in the past. . . . A statute designed
> to establish a color-blind and gender-blind workplace has thus
> been converted into a powerful engine of racism and sexism.
> . . . The irony is that [the Johnsons of this country] — predomi-
> nantly unknown, unaffluent, unorganized — suffer this injustice
> at the hands of a Court fond of thinking itself the champion of
> the politically impotent. I dissent [emphasis in original].[4]

Scalia imputes "racism" to affirmative action because it reduces the advantages of members of the white race. He imputes "sexism" because it reduces the advantages of members of the male sex. Scalia calls blacks and women "favored groups," and whites and males "nonfavored groups." In Scalia's view, the agency, in being persuaded by the affirmative action officer to override the results of the regular promotion process and to put Diane Joyce into the dispatcher slot, was treating not only Paul Johnson the individual but the white male "group" unfairly.

The agency had males in possession of all of the 238 skilled crafts positions and females in possession of not a single one. That staffing pattern does not suggest that the agency was already the "gender-blind workplace" that Scalia tells us the statute was designed to establish. When Diane Joyce was put ahead of Paul Johnson, the male sex's share of those jobs was reduced to 237 out of 238. The story of Joyce's effort to get a crafts job, which extended over five years and was successful only because of an affirmative action plan, shows how poor the opportunities for qualified women would have been in the plan's absence. The agency's affirmative action plan prescribed as a goal that women be placed in 3 of the expected 55 openings per year in that job category. Without the goal in place, and without the activities of the affirmative action officer, it is unlikely that any women would have been so placed.

The argument that the male sex was given a "disfavored" status by the agency's plan would be valid only if one believed that women's lack of merit is so universal for such not-very-demanding jobs that men would obtain 100 percent of them under a fair hiring system. Men did have their advantages reduced by the plan—that is, the degree of favor that had allowed them up to that point to retain a complete monopoly of certain jobs was reduced. That was the plan's whole point.

But what about Paul Johnson, the particular individual who missed out on the dispatcher's job? What can we say about him, and the possible violation of his rights? Paul Johnson was chosen for the dispatcher vacancy under a largely subjective system that gave great scope for the personal predilections of the decision-makers to influence the result. That system had not allowed a single female ever to occupy such a job. Johnson had tied for second place in the original ranking. The fact that he was preferred to the male candidate originally ranked first was not considered by anybody as dishonoring the principle of merit. It was only the displacement of the second-ranked person by the person ranked fourth that was contested on that ground. If Joyce had been a man, her selection for the job would not have been protested, and the lawsuit would not have been filed.

As we have seen, all nine finalists were judged well qualified. If all of the nine qualified candidates' names had been put into a hat and Diane Joyce's name had been drawn, Scalia would have had less ground to argue that Johnson was the victim of discrimination on account of his sex; he could have done so only by arguing that Joyce did not belong on the list at all. However, he might have criticized the names-in-the-hat method as a way of getting around the principle of merit and thus putting white males at a disadvantage. It is possible that no practical way of appointing Diane Joyce exists that would have passed muster with Justice Scalia.

If the names-in-the-hat method had been used, there would have been only a one-in-nine chance of desegregating this occupational category immediately. It is certainly reasonable to argue that the complete absence of women in all of the 238 jobs in this category called for the appointment of a woman when a good candidate showed up. A long delay would have wasted the chance for Joyce to serve as a role model, to demonstrate that one did not have to be a man to do the job well. Appointing a well-qualified woman to the skilled crafts group at the first opportunity brought nearer the day when segregation by sex would be a thing of the past. Our judgment of the morality of the exclusion of Paul Johnson depends on our judgment about the moral value of breaking the hold of sex segregation, versus the moral value of leaving the agency's "merit" system undisturbed.

Fairness and Elite School Admissions

The major justification for affirmative action in the workplace is its use as a systematic method of breaking down the current discrimination against African Americans and women. The desirability of diversity provides the strongest justification for affirmative action in college admissions. At a university, young people are trained for leadership roles in the professions and in public life. If we are to erase the deep racial cleavages that currently trouble us anytime soon, we cannot have campuses where black and Hispanic young people are rare or nonexistent. We cannot have white leaders who spent their college years in segregated institutions and never interacted with African Americans or heard their point of view.

Our campuses are in many ways the best parts of our country. For all their faults, they are places where people of intelligence gather to interact, to enjoy our literary and artistic inheritance, to enlarge their vision, to hone their critical sense, and to understand their place in life and their own potentialities. It would be tragic if on some campuses, and in some programs on our campuses, those African Americans who could perform there creditably were to be absent. A scientist who teaches at Brown says this about the talents and efforts of such students:

In twenty years of teaching at the university level, I have taught, advised and mentored a good many affirmative action admission students and not one of them could by any stretch of the imagination have been called an "underachiever." Most, in fact, were clearly overachievers who had made great strides despite the many obstacles that society and chance had placed in their paths. No, affirmative action doesn't allow anyone to get by on the color of his/her skin—we don't give affirmative action grades (except to athletes) no matter how the student got in. Affirmative action partly redresses a history of wrongs. We won't need it anymore once we have eliminated those wrongs.[5]

Campuses are also, of course, the places where the training and certification for the most prestigious, conspicuous, interesting, and lucrative careers take place. There is an obvious connection between the desegregation of higher education and the desegregation of the workplace: certain occupations cannot be entered without a credential from a college or university. Furthermore, there are important niches in certain occupations that anyone who has not passed through an elite university finds it much more difficult to occupy. So the elite institutions, along with all of the others, cannot remain segregated if we are to fully desegregate the country's jobs and to get black and female faces into all professional ranks, up to the highest.

It might be argued that achieving integration through affirmative action is appropriate in those parts of the labor market where outright discrimination still occurs but not in higher education, where discrimination in student admissions is no longer a problem. If affirmative action succeeds in the workplace, perhaps in the future a greater proportion of the sons and daughters (or grandsons and granddaughters) of the currently disadvantaged groups will have attended better elementary and high schools, grown up in better neighborhoods, and developed the hopes and sense of self-worth that will enable them to apply themselves in school and achieve admission to colleges and universities in greater numbers on a "fair" basis—on the same basis as whites and Asians.

In a sense, affirmative action programs on campus are a way to jump-start or accelerate the process of reducing racial dispari- ties—by getting more members of the current generation of minority young people into higher education and not waiting for the better academic and psychological preparation of future gen- erations that may follow when blacks gain a better position in the job market. Affirmative action in higher education admissions speeds the arrival of the day when racial disparities in status and economic success will have been greatly reduced. It makes allowances for something that admittedly is not the fault of black teenagers: the relatively poor preparation of many of them for higher education.

The major argument against affirmative action in higher edu- cation admissions is that it is unfair to those candidates with bet- ter test scores who are displaced to make room for the African American and Hispanic students. We have already met the assumption behind this argument in the field of employment— the assumption that institutions running selection processes are obligated to serve as arenas of competition among applicants and are not permitted to allow any consideration other than test scores to affect the outcome. For those who urge this point of view in university admissions, the nation's need to erase the effects of a shameful caste system count for nothing.

In fact, colleges and universities allow many considerations besides academic promise to affect admissions. Across the country, selective colleges and universities, which turn away many highly qualified students, admit several hundred athletes of low or nonexistent academic promise each year. These athletes, some black and some white, displace applicants—including black applicants—who have better test scores and better grades. Besides football and basketball players, schools give preference to runners, soccer players, baseball players, swimmers, and lacrosse players; the school must have them in order for their football and men's basketball teams to be allowed to compete in events sponsored by the National Collegiate Athletic Association (NCAA). It is sometimes said that one benefit of sports is to increase the number of blacks on campuses, that athletics constitutes a kind of affirmative action program that everyone can get behind—a two-for-one bargain. But many athletes have no interest in their studies, and no time or energy for them, and take the places of more academically motivated white and black students.

Many schools allow for regional diversity in their admissions process, giving preference to students from regions in which applicants are scarce. At Princeton or Yale, an applicant from Nebraska may be put ahead of an applicant from the East Coast with higher grades and test scores. Other applicants who are given special treatment in selective institutions are children of alumni. In 1988, 280 of 1,602 Harvard freshmen had fathers who had attended Harvard.[6] Of alumni children who apply, about 40 percent are admitted each year, while only 14 percent of non-alumni children are admitted. It is estimated that 240 more alumni offspring are admitted each year than would be the case if the parents' alumni status were not taken into consideration. Again, these 240 alumni children displace applicants with better grades and test scores. The Harvard Medical School announces in its application material that it gives preference to applicants who are the children of its graduates.

Applicants who are connected to influential or wealthy people—movie stars, other celebrities, multimillionaires—are also routinely given special preference. In addition, a university's administrative officers are known to ask for and to get special consideration for children of personal friends. The medical school dean's friends' children displace people with superior academic qualifications.[7]

Of course, two wrongs do not make a right. Preferential admissions of athletes, Nebraskans, offspring of alumni, and offspring of friends of the dean, if they are harmful, do not justify whatever harm affirmative action does. In fact, all such admissions do the same kind of harm—they displace candidates with better cognitive credentials, those whose talents run to academic pursuits rather than cross-country running or basketball. But just as affirmative action programs have benefits, these other special admissions practices have benefits too.

We can look at the benefits of each of these kinds of special admissions and see how they compare in value. The extra alumni

children are presumably admitted to reward the alumni for making financial contributions. (Have their places been bought, in a
sense?) The children of friends of the dean are there to give a nice
perk to the dean: they are one of the dean's fringe benefits, so to
speak. The athletes (or at least a few of them) provide entertain-
ment, boost school spirit, and in some rare cases, bring fame to
the school. If, however, the school is highly selective, it does not
need extra fame, since it has plenty of good applicants. By the laws
of mathematics, only half of the collegiate teams can win more
games than they lose in any season, and a much smaller proportion can have an outstanding number of wins. So the special
admission of the talented football and basketball players fails of its
ostensible purpose a good part of the time for almost all schools.
The assumption that sports teams generate revenue for schools is
unfounded in most cases.[8]

How do the reasons for affirmative action stack up against the
reasons for the other admissions? The reasons for affirmative
action are far more compelling: helping to cure this country's
racial cleavage, improving the parity of blacks in the job market,
encouraging blacks and whites to know each other on campus,
and giving a hand to the many young black people who grow up
in bad environments.

If we are going to eliminate special admissions to selective
schools, we should start with those special admissions that have
the weakest justification. Those who think that the special admission of alumni children and the other special admissions are more

justified than the special admission of African Americans should express that belief openly. If, on the other hand, they have merely overlooked the traditional beneficiaries of special admissions, they should redirect their drive for fairness in admissions to these higher-priority targets. After they have succeeded in eliminating special admissions for alumni children, athletes, Nebraskans, the wealthy, the well connected, and friends of the dean, they will have acquired the moral standing to raise their voices against affirmative action.

Compensation for Past Wrongs

Affirmative action for African Americans is sometimes justified as compensation for the mistreatment they have suffered in this country—two centuries of slavery followed by a century of intimidation and segregation in the South and poverty and discrimination throughout the country. There are two issues here: whether compensation is justified, and whether affirmative action is a good form of compensation.

Compensation has been made to other groups of people who have been unjustly dealt with. West Germany, a country of about sixty million people, has paid fifty billion dollars to Israel and to individual Jews as penance for the millions of people murdered, the forced flight, and the loss of homes and businesses that took place during the twelve years of Hitler's regime. The United States government has made monetary awards of twenty thousand dollars each to the Japanese Americans who were removed from their homes and normal lives and interned in camps during the four years the United States was at war with Japan. If those cases justify compensation, the suffering of blacks does also.

Compensation to African Americans for their suffering and that of their ancestors would be justified even if discrimination no longer existed and blacks had fair access to all jobs. It could take the form of money endowments to individuals and to black community organizations, as well as expressions of contrition and official commemorations of an evil time in our national life. On the analogy of veterans' preferences, preferences for government jobs could legitimately be part of the package.

However, affirmative action is amply justified apart from the compensation issue. As the wage and segregation data show, our labor market is still far from giving blacks fair access. Affirmative action is needed to fix that. While it partially redresses the crimes of the past, its main purpose is to cure a sickness in the present.

The Illusion That Blacks Always Win

In their talk of fairness, the foes of affirmative action focus on two individuals—a black person and a white person—competing for a job. The black person in their story is poorly qualified for the job. The white person is highly qualified, has worked very hard to get himself qualified, and is innocent of any wrongdoing toward this black person or any other. Most likely, the white person is from a

poor family and the black person grew up in comfortable circum-
stances. Affirmative action, its foes would have you believe, has
turned the labor market into a succession of contests between
pairs of individuals like these. In each contest, the undeserving
black person is declared the winner and gets 100 percent of the
prize, while the deserving white person is left with nothing. With
this perennial outcome, the situation has become pretty hopeless
if you are a white man. With white males depicted as losing in
each of these matchups, one may get the impression that the white
male group has suffered severely from affirmative action.

The evidence of how the labor market "contests" actually come
out—who is getting seats on the "good jobs bus"—shows, of
course, a quite different picture. There has been some desegregation since the 1960s, but as we have seen, many jobs in many
workplaces remain segregated. In the wages they earn, black people and white women are still far behind white males of similar
education and experience. Members of the white male group continue to win almost all of the contests for the best jobs in each of
the major occupational groups in most workplaces.

Affirmative action's removal of white men's privilege of exclusive
access to high-paying jobs does inflict losses on white men. The
foes of affirmative action fixate on those losses and ignore the reasons they are necessary, desirable, and fair. Foes pay no attention to
the losses of those individuals who, in the absence of affirmative
action, have been excluded because they are black or female.

The press has spotlighted the loss of privilege of certain white men and rendered invisible those black individuals who are cut out when white privilege is allowed to persist. One suburban county adopted an affirmative action program to desegregate its fire department, which had a history of total segregation by race. Some of the rejected white applicants organized a demonstration and invited the press. The local newspaper ran a photograph of the group of rejected white candidates across the street from the headquarters of the fire department, gazing at it mournfully and reproachfully. No pictures ever appeared in that newspaper showing the far larger group of blacks who for years had been rejected from firefighter jobs by a selection system rigged to exclude them. Able blacks had been excluded in favor of less qualified or equally qualified whites. The invisibility of the blacks who have been excluded by discrimination promotes the topsy-turvy view that whites are victims and blacks are in a privileged position in our society—that blacks have been "given too much."

Is Affirmative Action a Zero-Sum Game?

Would every gain for blacks and other minorities under affirmative action spell an equal loss for whites? Will men lose to the extent that women gain? If there were a rigidly fixed number of "good" jobs and "bad" jobs, then every time a "good" job was assigned through affirmative action to a black or a woman, a white man would be forced into a "bad" job.

It is not necessarily true, however, that the number of "good" jobs is fixed. The segregation of jobs by race and sex encourages employers to structure jobs earmarked for minority people and women as "bad" jobs. Since such people are not considered promotable, their job duties are restricted as much as possible to routine tasks. Jobs with duties that carry valuable on-the-job training opportunities tend to be earmarked for white males, who are understood to be eligible for higher responsibilities and whose training would be of potential benefit to the employer.

A breakdown in job segregation by sex and race would spread interesting duties, opportunities to learn, and opportunities for promotion to the incumbents of many currently "bad" jobs. For instance, if secretaries were integrated by sex they would be viewed—as they should—as potential management material. If secretarial jobs did become a way into management, secretaries would be more respected for their skills. Their jobs would be likely to be higher-paying as employers became interested in retaining good people who might be promotable. In the nineteenth century, when men held all the secretarial jobs, serving as a secretary was an excellent way to start a career.

Many of the jobs blacks now have are dirty, and some are dangerous. Like women's jobs, most of these jobs are treated by employers as dead ends. When blacks have greater mobility and are not restricted to a certain set of jobs, employers will have to improve such jobs to keep workers in them.

In a competitive labor market, any job with disagreeable characteristics—dirt, danger, boredom, heavy physical demands, little chance to pick up skills that would lead to promotion—should command higher pay than a job requiring equivalent skills that does not have such characteristics. In practice, with the high degree of race and sex segregation in the labor market, the jobs that pay badly are also bad in other ways. Employers can structure them that way because they know that they have a captive group of workers whose alternatives are largely closed off. Affirmative action, which breaks up the labor market monopolies that have been held by favored groups and makes blacks and women eligible for a greater variety of jobs, should have the effect of reducing the gap in pay and conditions between jobs that whites and blacks with a given education typically get. If affirmative action is successful, some whites will find themselves applying for jobs that hitherto only blacks have applied for, and some men will be applying for jobs that only women have previously held. But these jobs are likely to be better jobs than they would have been in the absence of affirmative action.

Finally, if we can reduce discrimination and segregation in the labor market, there will be gains outside of the labor market as well. All of us will benefit from revitalized central cities, lower crime rates, and fewer panhandlers, fewer homeless. It will be easier, more pleasurable, less guilt-inducing, and safer to live in a more just society.

six

Does Affirmative Action Hurt Its Intended Beneficiaries?

According to its opponents, affirmative action makes blacks lazy and unambitious, ruins the reputations of blacks who could make it on their own, and makes blacks angry at whites and whites angry at blacks. It has even been claimed that affirmative action promotes the popularity of anti-Semitic demagogues in the black community.

Supreme Court Justice Clarence Thomas, in the *Adarand* case, said:

So-called "benign" discrimination teaches many that because of chronic and apparently immutable handicaps, minorities cannot compete with them without their patronizing indulgence. Inevitably, such programs engender attitudes of superiority or, alternatively, provoke resentment among those who believe that they have been wronged by the Government's use of race. These programs stamp minorities with a badge of inferiority and may cause them to develop dependencies or to adopt an attitude that they are "entitled" to preferences.[1]

Just as all potent medications have side effects, affirmative action may well have some results that are bad for blacks or bad for women. To fight a war, you generally have to suffer some casualties; the war may also corrupt some of your own soldiers. As always, the issue is the balance of good and bad: are the bad effects of affirmative action so pervasive and so harmful that they outweigh whatever good might be accomplished?

Affirmative Action and White Behavior

Imagine you are an African American, recently hired for a job that you are perfectly competent to do well. When you start work, however, you find that some of your white colleagues resent your presence, shun you, and do nothing to help you learn the ropes. They do not explain their surly attitude to you, and you do not confront them. What caused this conduct? Were they simply ill disposed to accept an African American coworker? Or might affirmative action be responsible for their behavior, as some claim? Would those white workers have treated you well if the company did not have an affirmative action plan? In other words, did the company's affirmative action plan transform your otherwise congenial and fair-thinking white coworkers into mean-tempered bashers of their black colleague's abilities?

Nobody knows how often black workers who are put into all-white work groups receive hostile treatment, because such information has not been collected systematically.[2] That kind of behavior is probably far from rare. It can make life miserable for the new black employee, sometimes causing him or her to quit or fail. The motive behind at least some hostile behavior is to maintain the segregation that some white workers prefer.[3]

It is not unusual for women placed in previously all-male job crews to be received with hostility out of similar motives. Margaret S. Coleman, who was taken on in a crafts job at a New York telephone company, said this of her experience:

> People don't have a real understanding of the stress involved in being the woman who integrates a job. This stress is incredibly wearing and exhausting. She is in a situation where there is a wall of humanity antagonistically looking at every blemish, and the first sign of weakness is exploited to the max. I wonder how many men would make it if they would see such hate in the eyes of their assessors![4]

Sometimes the hostility takes the form of sexual harassment.[5]

There has been no research on the treatment of black employees in workplaces with and without affirmative action plans. Lacking research of this type, we cannot reliably distinguish instances of previously benign whites being turned ugly by affirmative action from those in which the whites were not benign to begin with. Thus, we have to conclude that this apparently potent accusation against affirmative action is not based on substantial information. It has been created by some of affirmative action's detractors, with a few anecdotes and some "common sense" serving as raw material. Affirmative action may sometimes be hurtful in the way these detractors claim, but we do not know how often. Pending some definitive research, some anecdotes and some common sense can testify for the defense of affirmative action as well.

I witnessed an incident in which a new African American employee, hired through an affirmative action program, had to face surly coworkers. It occurred when the University of Maryland Economics Department hired its first black secretary while I was a professor there. The three white secretaries who were to be her coworkers campaigned hard against the hiring of this black woman, on the grounds of lack of competence. They never made it clear how they knew she was not competent, but they were quite certain on this point. Our chair was a considerate and gentlemanly older man, but not an enthusiast for racial integration. He took the white secretaries' opposition seriously and did not like to go against them. He quizzed our black candidate's two former employers for twenty minutes each in a vain attempt to find some negative information about her. Without the pressure of affirmative action, she would certainly never have been hired: his reluctance, plus the white secretaries' all-out opposition, would have been decisive. But our chair was a team player when it came to dealing with the university administration, so the black candidate was hired.

Our white secretaries were not haters. I suspect they feared damage to their self-image if they belonged to a work group that included a black person. After she came aboard, their conduct for a time was rather poor. They talked to her as little as possible and did not invite her to join their lunch group. The black secretary tolerated their behavior with seeming serenity and held her peace, since the job was a relatively good one for her and she wanted to keep it. In the matter of competence, our new secretary was not the best, but neither was she the worst. The white secretaries were really decent people, and after a month or so they relented. Perhaps they also realized that she was there to stay, and that nothing could be accomplished by continuing their hostility, which I would guess was hard on their consciences. Thereafter, the four of them worked together normally.

Where was the balance of the good and the bad in this incident? The biggest plus was that a black woman got a job that would not otherwise have been offered to her. The opposition to her appointment shows that race did handicap her, and our affirmative action program redressed that. Our department made a small contribution to the achievement of an integrated society.

Students and staff who came into our department's office saw a work group that was integrated by race, a relatively rare sight at that time.

On the bad side, our black secretary had to suffer being labeled incompetent, although she later was able to remove the label by demonstrating normal competence. She herself was clearly willing to bear the label if doing so was the price of getting and keeping the job. Given the opposition to hiring a black for the job, it is not clear that she would have been spared that label even if the affirmative action program had been kept a secret from the white secretaries, or if she had been hired in the absence of an affirmative action plan, assuming that to be possible. In this case, the good clearly outweighed the bad.

A similar case in the Economics Department at Harvard turned out less happily. Until the early 1980s, the Economics Department, like almost all other Harvard departments, had never had a black person or a woman as a tenured professor. Probably under some pressure, or in response to some incentive from the Harvard administration, the department looked around and found an African American whom it was willing to hire for a tenured professorship. He was Glen Loury, a very bright theoretician and full professor at the University at Michigan, with a Ph.D. from MIT. Apparently, Loury never was made to feel at home in the Harvard Economics Department and deeply resented that. He transferred to another Harvard department and eventually, after some unrelated difficulties, went to another university. In a letter published in the *New York Times*, Loury testified to his own injury by affirmative action; he has since campaigned against it. We have to believe Loury's word that he was made miserable. However, his diagnosis that it was affirmative action that motivated the actions that constituted his colleagues' unwelcoming behavior may not be as firmly based as his report of his own misery. Even in this case, the good outcomes for Loury of affirmative action may have outweighed the bad: his hiring by Harvard gave him a prominent platform for his views he would not otherwise have had.

The suspicion of their peers that they are not competent must be particularly galling to those women and blacks who feel (correctly or not) that they were chosen on the basis of their perceived merit and would have been chosen even in the absence of an affirmative action plan. Such people, who may themselves have come to believe the argument that affirmative action inevitably means the hiring of incompetent people, feel that the affirmative action program has ruined their career by causing them to be labeled incompetent. But the affirmative action plan from hell that turns otherwise congenial colleagues into suspicious nasties has not been documented in a real-life case and may be a myth.

If hostilities and suspicions toward competent black colleagues are generated by affirmative action, they may be temporary. In some cases, such as that of the black secretary hired by the University of Maryland Economics Department, the hostility may diminish as white coworkers come to know blacks as individuals, something that might never occur in the absence of affirmative action. In other cases, the hostility may prove intractable. However, intractable hostility itself testifies to the need for affirmative action programs if there is to be integration.

Sleeping Her Way to the Top

In the days before affirmative action for women, any woman who achieved any kind of success in the workplace was likely to be the subject of remarks that she had "slept her way to the top." In those days, sexual harassment was common, as it remains today. The people who made such remarks were not deploring the demands for sexual favors by those with power to promote. Those demands were an accepted fact of life. Rather, those who made those remarks were maligning both the morals and the competence of any woman who advanced.

Such abusive remarks undoubtedly made life and work more difficult for the women subjected to them. The people who made them were not friendly to women's success in the workplace, or even neutral about it. Many men—and women also—held sexist attitudes, were jealous, and intended the remarks to be damaging and hurtful. They were looking for a way to tear down competent women, destroy respect for them, reduce any authority they might have, and make them fail in their jobs. Now affirmative action has been seized on as a way to disparage women and blacks who get promoted, with similar motives.

When people make remarks about women "sleeping their way to the top" or claim that all or most blacks hired through affirmative action are incompetent, they are expressing their resistance to change and trying to ensure the failure of the beneficiaries of affirmative action. This kind of behavior, assuming that it is widespread, certainly reduces the benefits of affirmative action to its intended beneficiaries. In the absence of affirmative action, blacks and women would be spared some ill-natured comments, but they would also be likely to be doing less interesting work, at lower pay and with less chance at promotion. The sentiments and behavior of people who make such comments are exactly what make affirmative action necessary in the first place. Their misbehavior is not a valid argument that nothing should be done to counter the effect of their prejudices.

The Four Sons Who Were Not Ashamed

In 1991, the *Washington Post* ran a story about a successful small bank in Washington, D.C.[6] In the picture that accompanies the story, two of the bank's tellers, a black woman and a white woman, stand in their cubicles. Above them, posed on a balcony leading to the suite of executive offices, are the president of the bank and its four vice presidents, all white men. The five white executives on

Washington Post photograph by Bill Snead

the balcony are revealed in the accompanying story to be a father
and his four sons. The four sons look in the picture as if they were
posing for the photographer quite proudly, although they knew

that the picture and the facts of their family relationship would be in the newspaper. They apparently had little or no fear that they would be disgraced by having their filial relationship to the bank's president revealed to hundreds of thousands of people. Like the alumni children who receive special admission to Harvard, Yale, and Princeton, they probably had never been anxious that people might make hurtful speculations about whether they deserved the slots they occupied or were competent to fill them. They had no worry about accusations that the special hiring plan their dad used to staff the highest executive positions in the bank was unfair to those who might otherwise have had their jobs.

We do not hear warnings to rich and well-connected people that they should refrain from using their influence to get their children into exclusive schools or hired for good jobs. Nobody writes books telling rich people that if they persist in this behavior they will create doubts about the talents of all of the rich children and about whether they deserve their college degrees and jobs. Luckily for the rich and their children, people almost never think to be hateful to them.

Affirmative Action and Laziness

The opponents of affirmative action claim, again without evidence, that affirmative action makes its beneficiaries lazy. In the words of Shelby Steele, "Affirmative action . . . offers entitlements, rather than development to blacks. A preference is not a training program; it teaches no skills, instills no values. It only makes a color a passport. . . . [T]he worst aspect of racial preferences is that they encourage dependency on entitlements, rather than on our own initiative."[7] Glen Loury asserts that affirmative action discourages the acquisition of skills. In his analysis, anything that helps an unskilled worker get a job in an unskilled occupation decreases that worker's interest in learning a skill and going into a skilled occupation.[8]

These claims are not even mildly plausible. The opposite is far more plausible. Affirmative action should make training more attractive rather than less. Why should a black person aspire to go to business school if he or she has a very low chance of getting a job in management? Many of the jobs that have been reserved for white men and that affirmative action programs try to open up have good on-the-job training opportunities. Shelby Steele's evidence for his theory is a story about a black graduate school colleague who told Steele that he planned not to exert himself too much after he got his Ph.D. degree. The man was true to his promise, says Steele, and got a job as a college administrator. As any college professor will testify, college administrators do have pleasant and easy duties, high pay, high status, good parking spots, and lots of perks like all-expenses-paid travel to nice places. One reason their jobs have been made so nice is that most college administrators are, of course, white men. Steele's contempt for his black colleague's alleged loss of energy and low aspirations does not appear to extend to those white men.

Loury's worry seems to be something like this: if you give a black person who had been excluded from a truck driver's job for reasons of race a fairer chance to get a truck-driving job, he or she will be more likely to pass up a chance to become a lawyer. He seems to think that is a good reason not to fight discrimination in fields like trucking. Loury's argument, to the extent it works at all, works equally well against any improvement in the chances for an unskilled person—black or white—to make a decent living. By that logic, we should tax the wages of lower-paid unskilled workers extra heavily so they will be motivated to acquire skills. Affirmative action seeks to reduce the unfair exclusion of blacks and women from both skilled and unskilled occupations, so there is no reason to think it should make the latter occupations relatively more attractive. (Perhaps the reader is beginning to wonder about the appropriateness of Loury's appointment to the Economics Department at Harvard. But the reader should be informed that silly theories are no disqualification there, as long as they are expressed mathematically.)[9]

Exploring How Blacks Feel about Affirmative Action

The opponents of affirmative action, particularly those who warn blacks that affirmative action will put them at grave disadvantage, have dominated the public discussion of the issue. In an attempt to see what some young blacks think about affirmative action, Sandra Tangri and I asked a group of fifty-two black college students to tell us how they thought affirmative action might affect them.[10]

We first asked the students to imagine themselves working in a job they had gotten without the benefit of affirmative action, a job in which they were doing well. Then their company decides to start an affirmative action plan. The students were asked to agree or disagree with a series of statements about the effect on them of that affirmative action plan. Their responses, given in table 6.1, show that some would worry about possible negative effects: about 20 percent of the students expressed anxiety about being typed as not competent because of the existence of the affirmative action plan (statement 6). However, a large majority would favor their employer starting such a plan. Seventy-five percent agreed with a statement favoring the affirmative action plan (statement 9). Only 4 percent disagreed; the rest apparently were undecided.[11]

The students were next invited to put themselves in the place of someone applying for a job at a company with an affirmative action plan (see table 6.2). Only 11 percent said they would pass up a job offered through an affirmative action plan (statement 9); another 6 percent were undecided. Only 12 percent would give up a job gained thanks to affirmative action for one that did not involve affirmative action but was somewhat less advantageous (statement 8).

By a majority of 64 percent to 12 percent, the students thought that affirmative action did more good than harm; 24 percent said they believed it made no difference. However, 82 percent thought that its abolition would make it harder for African Americans to get jobs. Only one of the fifty-two students who participated

Table 6.1

Opinions of Black Students Regarding the Effects of Affirmative Action on Black Job Incumbents

The purpose of this questionnaire is to find out how African Americans feel about *affirmative action*. You are asked to think about how affirmative action would be likely to help you or hurt you in various job situations.

Situation I: In this case, you have a job in a company that has never had an affirmative action plan. You got your job because you were clearly the best applicant. There are very few African Americans at your level or above—only you and one other person. You have been doing well, and seem to be well liked. The company wants to increase the number of African American employees, and has decided to start an affirmative action plan. What would you think about that?

	disagree	agree	undecided
1. I would be worried about the plan's effect on me.	58%	27%	15%
2. I think they could probably find quite a few really good African American applicants.	8	79	13
3. I would be glad that there will be more African Americans around.	0	92	8
4. I would be worried that they might hire African Americans who wouldn't work out.	60	17	23
5. Since there are plenty of mediocre whites on the payroll, I wouldn't be worried about a few mediocre blacks.	42	33	25
6. I would fear that some white coworkers would think I had been hired through affirmative action, and couldn't do the job. My chances for respect would go down.	60	19	21
7. If even one mediocre African American were hired, my future would be threatened.	83	6	11
8. I'd be glad to help the company find promising African Americans to hire.	4	88	8
9. On the whole, I would favor establishing the affirmative action plan.	4	75	21

Data are from a survey conducted by the author and Sandra Tangri.

Table 6.2

Opinions of Black Students Regarding the Effects of Affirmative Action on Black Job Applicants

The purpose of this questionnaire is to find out how African Americans feel about *affirmative action*. You are asked to think about how affirmative action would be likely to help you or hurt you in various job situations.

Situation II: In this case, you are looking for a job. You answer an advertisement and are told about a job that sounds quite good. You feel confident that you could do well at it. You are offered the job. You find out that the company has very few African American employees and has recently instituted an affirmative action plan. You guess that the plan might have played a part in your being offered the job. What would your reaction be to this offer?

	disagree	agree	undecided
1. I would welcome the chance for such a job, to show what I could do.	0%	89%	11%
2. I would rather be considered only on merit, even if that lowered my chance for an offer.	46	21	33
3. I would accept the job, if it was the best offer I could expect.	6	71	23
4. I would take the job, but I would worry that my white coworkers would think I was unqualified.	56	21	23
5. The people doing the hiring have not judged African American applicants fairly in the past, and that's why the company has so few of them.	11	56	33
6. I would expect that most of the white employees would treat me fairly, and accept me if I do good work.	35	42	23
7. If even a few of my white coworkers doubted my abilities, that would make things very hard for me on the job.	52	27	21
8. If I had another offer in a company where affirmative action wasn't an issue, I would take the other offer, even if it weren't quite as good as the one I could get through affirmative action.	61	12	27
9. I would probably pass up any job offered because of affirmative action, no matter how good.	83	11	6

Data are from a survey conducted by the author and Sandra Tangri.

claimed to have personal knowledge of anybody who had been hurt through affirmative action, and 46 percent said they knew of people who had been helped.

Affirmative Action and Anger

One claim made against affirmative action is that the program's very existence is taken by blacks to be an admission on the part of the white community that it has victimized blacks. This evidence of their victimization supposedly makes blacks angry and therefore susceptible to the rhetoric of extremists such as the anti-Semitic demagogue Louis Farrakhan. Shelby Steele, the leading exponent of this chain of reasoning, goes on to argue that the presence of angry anti-Semites in the black community creates a vicious circle by deceiving the white community into thinking that it needs to continue affirmative action to prevent even more anger from developing.[12]

There obviously is a great deal of black anger in this country, but the connection that Steele draws between affirmative action and black anti-Semitism, and his general point about the connections between oppression, remedies for oppression, and anger, are, when examined, quite implausible. First, blacks' discovery that they were oppressed did not have to wait for the appearance of affirmative action programs. The people who took part in the civil rights agitations of the 1950s and 1960s knew the score, and black people continue to be aware of oppression simply through living their lives. The frequency of gross police misconduct toward

African Americans is known to everybody. The humiliating treatment that even well-dressed blacks receive in stores and in their own workplaces perennially demonstrates to blacks that some whites, including some whites in influential positions, are racists.[13]

Second, when a problem is perceived, are we all supposed to just forget it? Are we to adopt the principle that we must never do anything about any problems we see because the people we are trying to help will get angry that the problem has not yet been fixed and will then act irrationally? That principle would condemn us to total immobility in all arenas, not just that of racial unfairness. One could more plausibly argue that oppression that is allowed to continue with no attempt at a remedy produces more anger than openly acknowledged oppression for which a remedy is being attempted.

Affirmative action does arouse anger among some whites, and this reaction does hurt blacks. Some of that white anger is whipped up by the foes of affirmative action, who then proceed to say that white anger is another bad effect of affirmative action. But some of the anger comes from whites who think, correctly or not, that they have been passed over for jobs or promotions because of affirmative action. Unfortunately, any advance, through any method, that gives a black a job that a white wanted and might have had may arouse resentment in the white person displaced, especially if he or she thinks that blacks are not good enough to deserve access to such jobs. If we were to avoid any degree of white resentment, we could accomplish nothing.

seven

Opinions Pro and Con

Overwhelmingly, people opposed to affirmative action have garnered more attention than people in favor of it. Republican politicians, with some honorable exceptions, have waged an aggressive campaign against it. Best-selling books by conservative blacks have argued that such programs do blacks great harm.[1] President Clinton has come to the defense of affirmative action, but most Democratic politicians have been silent. Pollsters asking for opinions about "preferences" to make up for "past discrimination" have reported lopsided majorities expressing opposition.[2] As a result, most people are probably under the impression that affirmative action has little support. In many circles it probably takes some courage to say you are in favor of it.

As we have seen, many employers still run workplaces where each type of job is totally segregated by race or sex. The first part of this chapter reports on a small-scale survey of opinions about what should be done in such workplaces. A considerable majority of respondents favored remedial action of some sort. Slightly more than half supported specific hiring programs aimed at ending the segregation. Those who were not in favor of affirmative action gave answers suggesting that they were opposed to it, not because of their passion for fairness or because they wanted to spare blacks the shame of being "affirmative action babies," but because they did not want to see the advantages of males or white people dismantled. That is a point of view that is never openly articulated when affirmative action is debated. It is out there, though.

The second part of this chapter looks at the stance of the American business community on affirmative action, and offers some explanations of why a cadre of business executives in large corporations has been highly active in its favor. The business community is usually impatient with federal regulation, yet it lobbied to retain the government's affirmative action programs during the Reagan and Bush presidencies and probably was responsible for saving them from extinction. This attitude may derive from a desire to have a free hand in recruiting from the more diverse labor force of the future, and from a worry about the fate of the country if racial divisions are not solved.

The Scenario of the Acme Company's Hiring Process

To analyze why people are for or against affirmative action, I asked a group of 173 mostly white undergraduates at American University, where I teach, to read a scenario describing the fictitious Acme Company. Half of the participants got a version of the scenario that described a firm that had never hired a single black worker for a certain type of well-paying blue-collar position. They were given a menu of possible actions the firm could take to change its hiring behavior and were asked which, if any, they favored. They were also asked for their reactions to a series of statements that probed their ideas about the reasons no blacks worked at Acme, and their attitudes toward changing that. The other half of the participants were asked for their reactions to a version of the scenario in which the firm had never hired women for such jobs.

The version of the scenario on black exclusion read as follows:

The Acme Company employs 301 machine operators, who operate large machines used in construction, such as bulldozers and cranes. Acme pays them $523 a week, which is good pay for a person without a college education. The personnel manager is concerned that the company has never hired a black in this job. The law says the company has to treat blacks and whites fairly, and he wants to make sure the company is hiring in a fair way.

A machine operator for Acme needs the kind of ability and judgment that an excellent car driver has. The person also needs a sense of responsibility, since careless mistakes could be costly and dangerous. All special training can be given on the job.

Acme had 23 vacancies last year, about 2 a month. Each time there is a vacancy, the employees are asked to spread the word, and an ad is put in the newspapers. Those who apply are given an aptitude test and an interview. The personnel department is then supposed to pick the best applicant.

The company, which is in a city that is half black, got applications last year for the machine operator vacancies from 440 whites and 45 blacks.

Acme's personnel manager looked back at what had happened to the black applicants. He found that they had done about as well as the white applicants on the aptitude test. However, most of the black applicants did not make a good impression on the interviewers. No black had been selected as the best candidate for any of the 23 vacancies, although for one of the vacancies a black had been rated third best.

Remedies Endorsed by Respondents

After reading the scenario above, respondents were presented with a list of five possible remedies and asked which, if any, they favored. The remedies and responses to them are displayed in table 7.1. The option of endorsing none of the specified remedies

Table 7.1

Percentage of Respondents Endorsing Suggested Remedies for Occupational Segregation by Sex or Race

	Respondents endorsing this remedial action, when the scenario depicts:	
	segregation by sex	segregation by race
R1. The personnel manager should remind the interviewers to be careful to be fair to women (blacks). He should tell them that men and women (blacks and whites) have an equal right to be considered for machine operator jobs.	84%	89%
R2. The personnel manager should try to find ways to encourage more female (black) candidates to apply, with a goal of doubling the number of female (black) applicants.	52	69
R3. The personnel manager should encourage the interviewers to hire at least a few of the women (blacks) who have been judged competent to perform the job.	30	31
R4. For the next few years, the personnel manager should try to fill at least 10 percent of the vacancies with women (blacks) who have been judged competent to perform the job.	34	32
R5. To break the pattern of an all-male (all-white) work force, the personnel manager should ask the interviewers to find competent women (blacks) and hire them for the next five vacancies.	16	15
Some action (one or more of R2-R5)	77	87
Some hiring action (one or more of R3-R5)	55	54
Numerical goals (one or more of R4-R5)	44	38

Data are from a survey conducted by the author.

with the exception of exhortation to be fair was taken by only 11 percent of those responding to the race-segregation scenario, and by 16 percent of those responding to the sex-segregation scenario.

Action by the firm to increase the number of black applicants drew approval from 69 percent of respondents, while the same remedy in favor of women drew only 52 percent approval. This difference reflects the sentiments of a body of male respondents who saw no urgent need to break down segregation by sex. In all, 54 percent were in favor of at least one activist hiring policy to reduce racial segregation;[3] 38 percent favored at least one of the two remedies that called for numerical goals. Those responding to the sex-segregation scenario endorsed numerical goals to a similar extent.

Attitudes toward Job Segregation by Race

Those responding to the race-segregation scenario were presented with a series of eight statements, shown in table 7.2, designed to throw some light on why they took the position on affirmative action that they did. Statements 2 and 6 were designed to test the extent to which respondents would endorse the explanations for occupational segregation commonly given by the opponents of affirmative action—that blacks do not occupy certain jobs because they lack the qualifications or are unwilling to take them. Respondents who agreed with these statements were in effect exculpating the company from discrimination and saying that blacks themselves were responsible for their underrepresentation. However, only a small minority of respondents were willing to endorse this line of thinking.

Table 7.2

Responses to Statements about the Exclusion of Blacks in the Workplace
(percent of respondents giving each answer)

	disagree	agree	undecided
S1. The Acme interviewers would probably have felt uncomfortable hiring a black as a machine operator.	28%	41%	30%
S2. Very few blacks would really be willing to do those kinds of jobs, and that's why you don't see blacks holding them.	82	6	12
S3. Things would be a lot better in this country if blacks had more of the well-paying jobs like the ones at Acme.	24	38	38
S4. The Acme interviewers probably tried to give the black candidates a fair shake.	44	30	25
S5. Putting blacks on a job of this kind might be disruptive, and the company has a right to be concerned about that.	84	9	7
S6. The Acme jobs are not the type that a lot of blacks would do well at, and that's why blacks don't have them.	94	2	4
S7. Lots of people could perform the machine operator job well.	9	81	10
S8. Despite the complete lack of blacks, Acme should not hire even a well-qualified black if it has a white candidate whom the interviewer thinks is better.	53	30	17

Data are from a survey conducted by the author.

Respondents were asked to say whether they considered greater equality for blacks in employment to be a good thing "for the country" (statement 3). Opinion was sharply divided: as might be expected, agreement with this statement was correlated with willingness to adopt special hiring procedures to break racial segregation.[4] By more than two to one, those who agreed that ending segregation would be good for the country favored special hiring procedures to increase the employment of blacks. Those who disagreed opposed special hiring procedures for blacks by almost four to one.

Since the overwhelming majority of respondents, including those who opposed affirmative action, had declared blacks willing and able to perform in the Acme jobs, we can conclude that many are opposed to affirmative action because they disagree with its aims rather than because they believe it is unfair.

Attitudes toward Job Segregation by Sex

A majority of those responding to the sex-segregation scenario endorsed the position that women were willing to do the job at Acme and had the necessary ability, although the majority was smaller than the one that endorsed the willingness and ability of blacks (see table 7.3). Of the respondents, 30 percent agreed with statement 5: women on the job might be disruptive, and the company had a right to be concerned about that. These respondents were essentially saying that it is reasonable to exclude women, and that sex discrimination is not necessarily a bad thing. Of those responding to the race-segregation scenario, only 9 percent gave a comparable answer; apparently more people are comfortable endorsing discrimination on account of sex than are comfortable endorsing racial discrimination.

Table 7.3

**Responses to Statements about the Exclusion of
Women in the Workplace
(percent of respondents giving each answer)**

	disagree	agree	undecided
S1. The Acme interviewers would probably have felt uncomfortable hiring a woman as a machine operator.	19%	70%	11%
S2. Very few women would really be willing to do those kinds of jobs, and that's why you don't see women holding them.	51	37	12
S3. Things would be a lot better in this country if women had more of the well-paying jobs like the ones at Acme.	34	37	29
S4. The Acme interviewers probably tried to give the women candidates a fair shake.	40	25	36
S5. Putting women on a job of this kind might be disruptive, and the company has a right to be concerned about that.	63	30	7
S6. The Acme jobs are not the type that a lot of women would do well at, and that's why women don't have them.	71	15	14
S7. Lots of people could perform the machine operator job well.	5	82	12
S8. Despite the complete lack of women, Acme should not hire even a well-qualified woman if it has a male candidate whom the interviewer thinks is better.	36	53	10

Data are from a survey conducted by the author.

Male and female respondents differed considerably in their opinions on affirmative action to end women's exclusion. Only 20 percent of male respondents thought the country would be better off if more women were in jobs like those at Acme, whereas 53 percent of the women thought so.

Interpreting the Survey Results

Conventional polls ask questions like, "Do you think that blacks and other minorities should receive preference to make up for past discrimination?" This kind of wording gives the respondent no information about the context of such "preferences" or about whether the "past discrimination" is over and done with or still in effect. The conventional poll thus allows the respondent free to construct mentally his or her own scenario and respond to that. Some respondents will think up a scenario that involves jobs requiring rare and specialized qualifications and in which discrimination is a thing of the distant past. Those respondents can then reason that most blacks and women could not do such jobs, and that affirmative action would result in the appointment of unqualified people. Responses to the vaguely worded questions posed in conventional polls are usually 75 percent "no."[5]

Respondents to the survey about the Acme Company did not have the same freedom to assume that the exclusion of blacks (or women) was justified. The scenario specified that the job in question required minimal talents—talents that are possessed by a large proportion of the population, white and black, male and female—and that all the required skills could be picked up through on-the-job training. The company's failure to hire any blacks could not easily be explained away by their lack of qualifications. Acme's process of evaluating candidates, as depicted in the scenario, depended a great deal on subjective judgments, allowing conscious or unconscious bias to operate. The people making the decisions had a track record of totally excluding all but white (or male) candidates. It would have been very difficult for any reasonably thoughtful person to imagine that blacks (or women) had been completely excluded for innocent reasons. Nor could that thoughtful person imagine that the hiring process would not continue to reproduce all-white (or all-male) work crews unless something in the hiring process changed.

A questionnaire of the type I used will obviously elicit more answers that are friendly to affirmative action than the one-sentence inquiry typically used by pollsters. What, then, is the "true" state of public opinion? There are many real-life situations that resemble the Acme scenario, and opinions about what to do about them are of interest. On the other hand, a survey on affirmative action that does not provide the respondents with a specific scenario to react to is meaningless, because the interpreter of the results cannot know what situation respondents were thinking about when they weighed in for or against affirmative action. They may be against affirmative action in picking math professors, but for it in picking truck drivers.

Many of the respondents to the Acme scenario who opposed numerical hiring goals understood that Acme had engaged in unfair practices against blacks and women, and that there was no innocent reason why the company had excluded blacks and women from its well-paying jobs. These respondents simply felt that there was no need to rectify the situation. Such people are not against affirmative action because they want to uphold the fairness of a strict merit system (which certainly does not exist in companies with a history like Acme's); they are opposed to it because they are unsympathetic to the reason for affirmative action: curing discrimination and giving blacks and women a fairer share of the good jobs in this country.

Business Support for Affirmative Action

During the presidencies of Reagan and Bush, conservative administration officials attempted to abolish the affirmative action requirements imposed on firms that do business with the federal government. Quite remarkably, it was the business community that protested the abolition of affirmative action and succeeded in quashing the move each time it was attempted. The lobbying in favor of keeping the federal government's requirement that each contracting company have an affirmative action program was led by two groups financed by large corporations. One was the Equal Opportunity Advisory Council, which describes itself as "a nonprofit association composed of more than 270 companies dedicated to the establishment of nondiscriminatory employment practices."[6] The other was the National Association of Manufacturers. The U.S. Chamber of Commerce, much of whose support comes from smaller businesses, lobbied on the side of eliminating government affirmative action requirements.

As we have seen, the government has not rigorously supervised the affirmative action programs of private employers. It has left businesses free to decide for themselves how vigorous a program to mount and how fast to proceed with it. Those businesses that have implemented affirmative action programs have done so from a variety of motives—to gain access to able workers, to improve customer and community relations, and possibly to act on a sense of responsibility for the social health of the United States.

Business executives have become increasingly conscious of the fact that white men now make up less than half the workforce and that their share is shrinking. If employers continue to allow white men to maintain their traditional monopolies over large segments of the job market, they will be forced to recruit important elements of their workforce from a smaller and smaller proportion of all workers. One sentence in the Hudson Institute's *Workforce 2000* has apparently caught and held the attention of many corporate managers: "White males, thought of only a generation ago as the mainstays of the economy, will comprise only 15 percent of the net additions to the labor force between 1985 and 2000."[7] The Hudson Institute statement has focused managers' attention on the need to "manage" the increased diversity of the workforce. The share of white native-born men in the American workforce has been shrinking since 1950. By 1980 their share had dipped below 50 percent; by 1994 it was down to 41 percent. Government projections place the proportion of white men in the national workforce in the year 2005 at 38 percent.[8]

The main reason for the drop in the white male share has been the mass entry of women into the labor force. By 1994 women comprised 46 percent of the labor force. They are continuing to increase their labor force participation rate, while that of men continues to decline. A second, but smaller, source of the decline of the native-born white male share has been the influx of Hispanic workers. By 1980 there were 6.1 million Hispanic workers of both sexes in the United States. In 1994 there were 11.7 million, making up 9 percent of the labor force.

As total employment grows, the numbers of managers and skilled blue-collar crafts workers needed by employers also grow; these are the occupations white males have traditionally dominated. The continuation of that dominance in these occupations would mean greater competition among employers for an increasingly limited pool of white male workers. It would also result in a greater proportion of the managerial and crafts jobs being filled by the less talented white males, thus degrading productivity. At least some white and minority women and some minority males have talents and qualifications that are superior to those of the white males who would have to be hired if the former were excluded.

A failure to consider blacks and women for the better jobs has always resulted in the elimination of good candidates from contention. Even so, restricting the field of candidates to native-born white men could be tolerated when they constituted 60 percent of the labor force; that restriction has looked less tolerable as the share of conventional candidates sinks below 40 percent.

Some business leaders are also sensitive to the striving of women for greater respect and improved access to the better jobs. Anyone who wants to appear to be progressive and modern cannot advocate traditional sex roles. Business organizations that confine women to traditional jobs cannot maintain an up-to-date image—the image most business leaders want for their organizations. If business executives have families typical of white married men, almost one-third of those with children have daughters only. Many such fathers have proven to be advocates for equality for women, at least in the managerial and professional jobs their daughters might aspire to.

It must be recognized, however, that the relatively reduced availability of white men will by no means guarantee a reduction in occupational segregation by sex and race. There will be more than enough white men to go around for the top jobs, if there is as bit of redefinition as to who is "white," and what the "top jobs" are. In twenty years, many young men of Asian and Hispanic origin will probably be considered acceptable for those "top jobs"— at least, to a far greater extent than their fathers have been. A continuation and intensification of affirmative action will be required if African Americans and women are also to become acceptable.

Typically, shifts in labor force composition in the past have led to a total shift of some job categories from one group to another rather than to a breakdown of segregation. The labor market has reacted very much like the urban residential real estate industry, which when faced with an influx of blacks or Hispanics has

expanded the ghetto rather than allowed the formation of integrated neighborhoods. The job of bank teller, formerly a segregated white male occupation, became largely female during World
War II and has remained so. Again, only affirmative action carries
the promise of desegregation.

Corporate Concerns about the Social Health
of the United States

Concern with the long-term social and political environment of
this country has also influenced business managers. In larger corporations, the top executives are likely to feel some responsibility
for the stewardship of the country, both because of the influence
they wield and because they understand that social and political
conditions affect the climate in which they operate. The more
thoughtful among them, especially those with international standing and contacts, feel ashamed about our unsolved problems of
race and poverty and the attendant crime, urban decay, unwed
motherhood, drug addiction, and demoralization. They know that
the United States has by far the worst record on child poverty and
on violence of any developed country. They worry that the antiso-
cial behavior of those who feel left out of mainstream America is
detrimental, even dangerous, to the society that constitutes the
corporation's environment, and they know that such behavior has
expensive consequences. They see that these problems have

caused the United States to lose standing in the world, and they understand that American business loses too in important ways.

The right-wing solution to our problems with race and the underclass would be to maintain a stern attitude toward those at the bottom, to deny welfare benefits, and to assign jobs strictly according to merit, with merit being assessed by those who have been assessing it all along. Those in the business world who reject this view see blacks' problems in the job market as a major cause of America's racial problem, and they see special programs to help put blacks into more and better jobs as a necessary part of the solution. They worry that America's racial problems, if allowed to continue and become further inflamed, could put the stability of the country into jeopardy.

Neither extreme left-wing nor right-wing movements have had lasting success in this country in the past. However, increasing tensions between the races, and the crime problems and resentments that such tensions bring, conceivably could fuel political movements that might endanger the country's basic institutions—institutions that business feels comfortable with. The larger the corporation, the more likely it is that its leadership feels some responsibility to conduct personnel policy in a way that is conducive to a healthy, socially unified United States.

eight

Alternatives to Affirmative Action

Some who favor the aims of affirmative action but worry that it cannot survive the growing political and legal attack from the right are pushing a substitute: "Just help people from disadvantaged backgrounds." The foes of affirmative action say, "Just enforce the laws against discrimination." In this chapter, we look at the strengths and weaknesses of some proposed alternatives to affirmative action. Some of these alternatives have value and should be used, whether affirmative action lives or dies. The question, though, is whether any of them, or any combination of them, would be sufficient to accomplish the difficult job of achieving fairness in the labor market if affirmative action does die.

Help to the Disadvantaged

The growing agitation against affirmative action has triggered a hunt for substitutes that would help the African American community but be more widely accepted than affirmative action. Some are suggesting programs that would single out for help people from disadvantaged backgrounds, regardless of their race or sex.[1] Since African Americans suffer from high rates of poverty, those promoting this strategy hope that such a program would help many of the same people who are targeted by affirmative action. Some white males would presumably be included in the program, perhaps making it less unpopular than affirmative action.

In practice, a black person might get a job that a white person might have had in the absence of such a program. However, that displacement of white for black would be done in the name of helping the disadvantaged rather than helping blacks. It might therefore pass muster with those who claim their opposition to affirmative action is based on abhorrence of any program that makes use of people's racial or ethnic identification.

Working out the details of such a program might be difficult. Certifying the background of those qualified to participate could be cumbersome and subject to fraud. Further, a majority of the poverty-stricken population is white non-Hispanic; African Americans constitute 28 percent of the poor.[2] African Americans might not get even 28 percent of the slots made available by such a program if there were no element of race-based selection. If these slots were valuable opportunities, white males might vie for them and win almost all of them unless care were taken to avoid such an outcome. There is a name for that kind of care: affirmative action. Whites already win most of the well-paying jobs that go to low-skilled people of modest backgrounds—over-the-road truck drivers, house painters, and the like. To prevent the program from freezing out blacks, formal or informal quotas for blacks in the program would have to be set up. But if that happened, the program would become race-based.

There is a more fundamental reason why a program for the disadvantaged would be a poor and inadequate substitute for affirmative action, which acts specifically to end segregation by race and sex. A program based on disadvantaged status would leave much discrimination-caused segregation intact. Consider the large law firm, with no active affirmative action program, that has never hired a woman or a black person as a lawyer. If it already has some white male lawyers who grew up in poverty, then presumably it has fulfilled its obligation under a program of helping the disadvantaged and would not feel a need to desegregate by race and sex. If it has no lawyers from a disadvantaged background, then it could take on some. If they all turned out to be white males, no complaint could be made on that score, provided no overt discrimination had been practiced.

A program to give special help to the disadvantaged might accomplish some good. While it would not do the job that affirmative action is designed to do, it would be a worthwhile companion program.

Enforcing the Laws against Discrimination

If we have laws to protect us against discrimination, what do we need affirmative action for? The answer, of course, is that the laws that prohibit something do not always do a good job of protecting us against it. Many people engage in practices forbidden by law—selling and using illegal drugs, being delinquent in child support payments—despite the laws against them. Laws alone are ineffective when the behavior that they forbid is not confined to a small part of the population, when the behavior goes on behind closed doors, when violations are difficult and expensive to prove, and when the penalties are not easy to apply.

All of these difficulties hobble the application of the laws against discrimination. The practices that result in a high degree of segregation by job are ingrained: they seem natural and right to many people. Many of them are sins of omission, such as a failure to include women and African Americans in the pool of people being considered for a job.

Whether discrimination has actually occurred in any particular case, and the extent of the damages suffered, have to be determined by filing a lawsuit in a federal court. The lawsuit can be brought by the injured workers or by the Equal Employment Opportunity Commission (EEOC). The EEOC has had the resources to bring to court only a tiny fraction of the thousands of complaints that are filed with it each year. The agency receives sixty-three thousand complaints of employment discrimination a year and brings suit in fewer than five hundred cases. During the years of the Reagan and Bush presidencies, the EEOC further limited its effectiveness by concentrating on suits on behalf of individuals. The agency generally avoided filing class action suits, in which the discrimination claims of large groups of employees are addressed in a single suit. Class action suits are the only ones that can cause employers adjudged to have discriminated under the Civil Rights Act to suffer substantial financial loss. They generate more publicity, lend themselves to statistical evidence, and also make it difficult for the employer to base a defense on the alleged bad behavior, incompetence, or peculiarities of those bringing the complaint.

Antidiscrimination lawsuits are not easy for plaintiffs to win, and even those who do win may wait many years before receiving redress. Court cases can drag on for decades without final resolution. In one case started in 1973, a group of women employees sued the U.S. Navy, claiming they had been discriminated against in pay and promotion because of their sex.[3] It took eight years before the federal judge in charge of the case made a decision, ruling in favor of the complainants. However, some issues remained to be ruled on, and that took five more years. It took still another five years for damages of $670,000 to be determined and awarded to the women by the court. However, even then the damages were not paid because the navy appealed the judgment to a higher court.

A group of eleven hundred women workers brought charges of

sex discrimination against the U.S. Information Agency (USIA) in 1977. In 1984, seven years later, a federal judge ruled that the women had suffered discrimination and were owed damages. The amount of money they were to be paid as damages had still not been determined by the end of 1992, and, of course, nothing had been paid. One of the reasons that the case against the USIA dragged on for so long was that so many women were involved. It is standard procedure in court cases to require a detailed assessment of the damages owed each individual, and this process is very time-consuming. At such hearings, the employer has an incentive to bring forward any derogatory information about each woman complaining of sex discrimination in order to justify her adverse treatment. Generally, no damages are paid until each individual's case has been dealt with. Paradoxically, the more systemic and thoroughgoing an employer's discriminatory conduct, and the greater the number of people victimized by that conduct, the longer the employer will be able to stave off making restitution.[4]

Another example of a long-running case involved blacks who worked in a unionized DuPont plant in Louisville, Kentucky, that manufactured plastics.[5] The black workers accused both DuPont and the union of running a seniority system that made it virtually impossible for them to transfer to better-paying jobs. In 1969 legal and administrative proceedings against the company resulted in some promotions for individual blacks. However, by the early 1970s, blacks—who constituted 30 percent of the population of Louisville—still held only 2 percent of the higher-paying blue-collar jobs in the plant. In 1973 the blacks again filed suit, charging that the seniority system was discriminatory.

In the DuPont suit, the case hinged on the employer's personnel records, which contained evidence of how the employees were treated. The complainants in the lawsuit had the right to ask the company to turn over to them relevant material from these files during the pretrial process called "discovery." In such cases, the employer will typically resist complying with all of the complainants' requests, and the judge decides what is relevant and must be turned over.

The DuPont case was marked by lengthy disputes over the extent to which the company had to comply with the complainants' demands for information about how vacancies were filled, and the court was slow to resolve them. Eventually, the company was required to turn over the information, but the company's lawyers had been able to protract the pretrial discovery process for almost two decades. They also filed numerous motions for dismissal of the case, each of which took time for the complainants to answer and time for the judge to decide. Over this period, four different judges were involved: the first judge withdrew from the case; the second died after working on it three years; the third died after working on it twelve years. Each change of judge occasioned further delay.

Judges are not all alike in their willingness to tolerate delays. The fourth judge to handle the case, known for his no-nonsense approach, quickly set a trial date, tried the case in four days, and

ruled a few weeks later that the black workers had been discriminated against. However, the company appealed, pushing off the
resolution still further into the future.

Most cases do not take nineteen years to get to trial, but cases
that last the better part of a decade or longer are the rule rather
than the exception. The length of time it takes successful plaintiffs
to achieve redress obviously discourages people from bringing
such cases. While these cases are in front of the court, the plaintiffs' lives and careers are "on hold." Since the EEOC can bring so
few cases, most complainants need to hire private lawyers, whose
up-front, out-of-pocket costs require that the complainants lay out
some money to reimburse them at the beginning of the case. Individuals pursuing discrimination complaints have had to liquidate
their assets and sell their homes to pay these expenses, many of
them in a losing gamble. In some lines of work, bringing discrimination charges makes the complainant unemployable when other
employers hear about the suit and want nothing to do with a
"troublemaker."

If an individual is willing to go ahead with a lawsuit charging
discrimination despite the difficulties, it is not easy to get a competent lawyer to take even a case that looks solid. The federal
judge to whom the case is randomly assigned may turn out to be
one of the many who are hostile to employment discrimination
complaints under the Civil Rights Act. Ordinarily, the largest part
of the lawyer's compensation comes at the end of the case, and
only if the lawyer has won the case. The length of time these cases

take is a powerful incentive for talented lawyers who have other alternatives to avoid getting involved in them.

A lawsuit, if successful, may result, after a decade or more, in restitution of lost wages for individuals who have been discriminated against, reimbursement of legal expenses, and possibly punitive damages. However, such monetary awards cannot repair much of the harm that discrimination and the lawsuit itself cause to the individuals involved. If the company contests the charge, it will dig up anecdotes that will put the complainant's performance and behavior in the worst light. Given the ordeal involved, people who feel they have been discriminated against are well advised to avoid lawsuits, and most do. Very seldom is the person reinstated to a position with the original employer commensurate with the position he or she would have held had the discrimination not occurred and the lawsuit not been brought. Nor can unclouded relations between the parties be restored. A sum of money cannot begin to compensate for the bitterness that being the object of discrimination engenders or for the loss of the opportunity to do more interesting work, develop one's talents, supervise others, or gain the self-esteem that comes from a smoothly developing career. Nor does the damage award compensate for the anxiety and time demands of being involved in a lawsuit with an uncertain outcome that will go on for a long and indeterminate period.

Lawsuits may have little direct effect on the employer's hiring, assignment, and promotion practices. The judge will not require the employer to discipline individuals who have been responsible for discriminatory acts, even egregious ones; such individuals may continue to play a major role in personnel decisions. When the complainant is an individual who no longer has a job with the employer and is represented by a private lawyer rather than an antidiscrimination agency of the government, no pressure will be brought to bear on the employer to make changes. Such a complainant, usually having left his or her job with the employer, no longer has a direct interest in changing the employer's personnel practices and is unlikely to expend time, money, and energy asking the judge to order systemic changes.

Even if lawsuits were much cheaper, quicker, and easier than they are, there would still be good reasons not to depend on them as a way to remove discriminatory practices from the workplace. The vast majority of people who are discriminated against have no way of knowing that this has happened to them. In most situations, rejected job applicants have no information that would enable them to judge whether their qualifications are better than those of the candidates selected. Those who have been hired but assigned to dead-end segregated positions, or passed over for promotion on account of their race or sex, are unlikely to pursue complaints unless they have a superior position outside the company lined up to go to and frequently not even then. Many employees are not even aware that segregation by race or sex on the job is wrong or illegal.

Finally, most people are not of a disposition to embark on a crusade for their rights; most are absorbed in everyday concerns about making a living, keeping their job, and having a reasonably pleasant relationship with bosses and coworkers. They know that accusations of discrimination would poison their relations with their employer, and with good reason they fear being blacklisted with other employers. For all of these reasons, it would be futile to depend on lawsuits to do the job of eliminating discrimination in our society.

Antidiscrimination lawsuits do have their uses. They have served to test the definition of what constitutes discrimination under the law and what does not. The courts have declared sexual harassment to be discriminatory. They have disallowed seemingly neutral tests that disproportionately screen out minority persons and women unless such tests are rigorously job-related. They have told employers they are discriminating when they exclude all women on the grounds that the "average woman" is in some respect inferior to the "average man," and when they exclude all blacks on the grounds that the "average black" is inferior to the "average white." Occasionally, a class action lawsuit brought on behalf of a sizable group of employees results in a large damage payment by an employer, alerting other employers to avoid the conduct that brought on the suit.

However, employers would make progress at a snail's pace if they moved only in response to lawsuits, opened up jobs only to those proven in a court of law to have been discriminated against, and changed only those procedures proven discriminatory in court proceedings.

Education and Training

Some of those who deplore affirmative action have argued that the way to solve the race problem in this country is to improve the qualifications of African Americans through training programs, in part by improving the schools black children attend. When blacks' qualifications are as good as those of whites, employers will want to hire them and the problem will end, according to this line of argument.

The disparity in educational and training opportunities for blacks and whites does need to be redressed. But those who advocate training instead of affirmative action ignore the fact that even now blacks and women with good qualifications do not do as well as white men in the labor market. Women college graduates earn little more on average than males with only a high school diploma.

Representing the education-improvement strategy as a solution that does away with the necessity for affirmative action puts off making improvements in the job situation for blacks until an indefinite future that may never come. It derails the drive to make employers hire more black people for jobs they can do well right now. Hundreds of billions of federal dollars have been spent on training programs for the disadvantaged over the last thirty years, but the results in terms of increased earnings for the trainees have not been impressive.[6]

Improving the qualifications of blacks will have limited effect unless employers treat equally qualified blacks and whites equally. The Urban Institute testing study and many studies based on census data show that blacks and whites with similar qualifications are not being treated equally by employers right now. The education-improvement approach ignores the fact that it is difficult to motivate young people to undergo training and take education seriously if they have little hope of getting a good job at the end of it. It also ignores the fact that blacks and women are largely excluded from much of the work for which unskilled persons are hired and given on-the-job training. Apprenticeship programs, which could provide an excellent way to integrate crafts occupations by sex and race, continue to be egregious offenders in restricting their benefits to white males.[7]

Better education should be part of our program for reducing racial and sexual disparities, and so should on-the-job training programs with slots reserved for blacks and women. Nevertheless, however well they augment programs to reduce discrimination, training and education programs cannot replace them.

Testing Programs

"Testing"—sending out carefully matched pairs of people of different races or ethnicities to apply for the same job—has been used to diagnose the extent of discrimination in the labor market. Programs of this type might be used also for enforcement purposes, to provide evidence against individual employers. A similar program has already been used in the housing field. Matched pairs have been sent to apply for apartments, and their disparate treatment has provided considerable evidence of discrimination. This evidence has formed the basis of successful legal moves against landlords who discriminate.[8] In the employment field, because repeated tests would be required to show that any particular employer was discriminating, the technique could be used only against employers with a sizable stream of vacancies. Testing of employers is a highly promising strategy against discrimination. It is no substitute for affirmative action but complements it. Affirmative action is the procedure that employers need to put in place to ensure that if they are tested, they are shown not to be discriminating.

Just Pray

The foes of affirmative action do not say, but certainly imply, that we should give up the effort to decrease labor market segregation by race and sex. They imply that everything is already fair enough. Those groups who currently do badly in the job market would presumably get the same consideration and have the same success as white males if they improved their qualifications and their behavior. At a recent Princeton University public policy conference, three panel members—a representative of the conservative Heritage Foundation, an African American foe of affirmative action, and a Clinton White House adviser—agreed on another strategy to improve the position of the disadvantaged. They all said that an increase in religious devotion on the part of the historically subordinate groups could provide an answer to America's social problems.

Some foes of affirmative action do not hold out much hope that even more prayer could improve matters. They tell us that no matter what African Americans do, they will always lag behind because their genes are of poor quality.[9] There is a large market for this kind of news; Herrnstein and Murray's *The Bell Curve* has sold hundreds of thousands of copies.

The evidence on the extent of segregation of jobs by race and sex shows that there are problems of discrimination in the labor market. If we attack those problems directly, we will be improving the incentive for young people—the ones now left out—to behave prudently and to get an education. If we do not, the exhortations to young people to be good and to study will continue to fall on many deaf ears. Prayer has never taken us very far in solving this country's race and poverty problems. Only an activist policy—with affirmative action as a prime ingredient—will do that.

Notes

Chapter 1. Thinking about Affirmative Action

1. Dee Dee Myers was Clinton's first spokesperson. For the list as of 1995, see Todd S. Purdum, "Desperately in Need of Winning Streak, Clinton Finds One," *New York Times*, May 7, 1995, p. 1.

2. Hugh Davis Graham, "The Origins of Affirmative Action: Civil Rights and the Regulatory State," in *Affirmative Action Revisited*, ed. Harold Orlans and June O'Neill, *Annals of the American Academy of Political and Social Science* S23 (September 1992): 50.

3. U.S. Bureau of the Census, *Statistical Abstract of the United States: 1994*, 114th ed. (Washington, D.C.: U.S. Government Printing Office, 1994), p. 546.

4. Data on Ford and other government contractors are based on company reports to the Equal Employment Opportunity Commission; see ch. 2, n. 31.

5. See Barbara R. Bergmann, "Curing Child Poverty in the United States," *American Economic Review* (May 1994): 76–80.

6. Others reject the use of the word *quota* in the context of affirmative action on the grounds that it falsely suggests an analogy between affirmative action goals and the quotas limiting the number of Jews admitted to elite schools prior to World War II. See the discussion of this issue in chap. 4; see also Gertrude Ezorsky, *Racism and Justice: The Case for Affirmative Action* (Ithaca, N.Y.: Cornell University Press, 1991), p. 38.

7. See Donald Tomaskovic-Devey, *Gender and Racial Inequality at Work: The Sources and Consequences of Job Segregation* (Ithaca, N.Y.: ILR Press, 1993), and Michael Fix and Raymond J. Struyk, eds., *Clear and Convincing Evidence: Measurement of Discrimination in America* (Washington, D.C.: Urban Institute Press, 1993).

8. Bureau of the Census, *Statistical Abstract of the United States: 1994*, p. 476.

9. See Frances K. Conley, "Why I'm Leaving Stanford: I Wanted My Dignity Back," *Los Angeles Times*, June 9, 1991, p. M1. See also Robin Herman, "Surgeon Denied Promotion Files Suit, Accusing Children's Hospital of Sexism," *Washington Post*, February 5, 1993, p. B5; and Elsa Walsh, *Divided Lives: The Public and Private Struggles of Three Accomplished Women* (New York: Simon and Schuster, 1995).

10. *Johnson v. Transportation Agency of Santa Clara County, Calif.*, 107 Sup. Ct. 1442 (1987).

11. U.S. Bureau of Labor Statistics, *Employment and Earnings,* July 1955, p. 155. "White men" in the bureau's terminology includes most Hispanics, who make markedly lower wages than non-Hispanic white men. The figure quoted is derived by removing the wages of Hispanic men from the average for "white men" and including them with all other labor market participants.

12. See James N. Baron, "Organizational Evidence of Ascription in Labor Markets," in *Equal Employment Opportunity: Labor Market Discrimination and Public Policy*, ed. Paul Burstein (New York: Walter de Gruyter, 1994), pp. 71–84.

13. Stephen L. Carter, *Reflections of an Affirmative Action Baby* (New York: Basic Books, 1991), p. 2 (emphasis in original).

Chapter 2. Is Discrimination a Thing of the Past?

1. Richard Morin and Sharon Warden, "Americans Vent Anger at Affirmative Action," *Washington Post*, March 24, 1995, pp. 1, 4.

2. Some of them are newly created jobs, and others are jobs vacated by people who have quit, been fired, retired, died, or been promoted. Between 1984 and 1994, the number of people employed grew from 105 million to 123 million, an average growth rate of 0.134 percent per month. Current data on the rate at which workers leave jobs are no longer available, but a rate of 0.8 percent per month is in line with previous estimates by the Bureau of Labor Statistics.

3. See Richard J. Herrnstein and Charles Murray, *The Bell Curve: Intelligence and Class Structure in American Life* (New York: Free Press, 1994). The chart on p. 490 purports to show the jobs blacks held, by occupation, as a percentage of the jobs they

deserved to hold, based on their cognitive abilities. Herrnstein and Murray maintain that they held 100 percent of the jobs they deserved in these two categories, in 1964 and 1967, respectively. They are silent on the subject of women.

4. Gunnar Myrdal, Richard Sterner, and Arnold Rose, *An American Dilemma: The Negro Problem and Modern Democracy* (New York: Harper Brothers, 1944). See also Herbert Hill, *Black Labor and the American Legal System: Race, Work and the Law* (Madison: University of Wisconsin Press, 1985).

5. Shelby Steele, "How to Grow Extremists," *New York Times*, March 13, 1994, p. E17.

6. Richard A. Posner, "Economic Analysis of Sex Discrimination Laws," *University of Chicago Law Review* 56 (1980):1311, reprinted in Mary Joe Frug, *Women and the Law* (Westbury, N.Y.: Foundation Press, 1992), pp. 297–307.

7. June O'Neill, "The Shrinking Pay Gap," *Wall Street Journal*, October 7, 1994, p. A10.

8. Weekly wages of full-time workers by race and sex are published by the U.S. Bureau of Labor Statistics in the periodical *Employment and Earnings*.

9. See Francine D. Blau and Lawrence M. Kahn, "Gender and Pay Differentials," in *Research Frontiers in Industrial Relations and Human Resources*, ed. David Lewin, Olivia S. Mitchell, and Peter D. Sherer (Madison, Wisc.: IRRA, 1992), p. 389.

10. For a simple explanation of this technique, see Barbara R. Bergmann, *The Economic Emergence of Women* (New York: Basic Books, 1986), pp. 76–82.

11. The estimate of the gaps based on the NLSY data were calculated by the author on the basis of material reported in

George Farkas, Paula England, Keven Vicknair, and Barbara Stanek Kilbourne, "Cognitive Skill, Skill Demand of Jobs, and Earnings among Young White, African-American, and Mexican-American Workers" (Dallas: University of Texas at Dallas School of Social Science, 1995). Farkas et al. bear no responsibility for these calculations. The estimated gaps based on census data were calculated by the author using U.S. Bureau of the Census tapes of the 1991 Current Population Survey. The census estimates are based on weekly wages, while the NLSY estimates are based on hourly wages, of employed persons working at least thirty-five hours per week. The wages were annualized by calculating pay for fifty-two weeks per year, and, in the case of the NLSY estimates, forty hours per week. Thus, these estimated gaps do not include the effect of the relatively high unemployment rates that blacks suffer, which are caused at least in part by discrimination in hiring. Details of the calculations are available from the author.

12. The lower chance that black adults had as children to have their cognitive talents nurtured was attributable in great measure to discrimination against the black community. However, lower cognitive skills are not themselves due to current employer discrimination. Therefore, differences in wages that can be traced to differences in cognitive skills should not be counted as part of the residual gap.

13. Mary C. King, "Occupational Segregation by Race and Sex, 1940–88," *Monthly Labor Review* 115, no. 4 (1992): 30–37.

14. See Donald Tomaskovic-Devey, *Gender and Racial Inequality at Work: The Sources and Consequences of Job Segregation* (Ithaca, N.Y.: ILR Press, 1993).

15. The survey did show that women had very poor representation in crafts jobs, and that both women and blacks were underrepresented in managerial and supervisory jobs.

16. Tomaskovic-Devey, *Gender and Racial Inequality*, pp. 30–37. Jobs with substantial numbers of males and females doing the same work were defined as ones held by 30–70 percent women. A national survey on sex segregation done in 1991 came up with similar findings. With a total absence of assignment based on sex or race, the percentage of people working only with members of their own race or sex would not be zero, because some job titles would have only a single employee, and some small groups would be single-sex or single-race by chance.

17. U.S. Department of Labor, "OFCCP Quick Facts" (Washington, D.C.: U.S. Department of Labor, n.d.).

18. A friendly reader has suggested that would not happen, because birthdays are not inherited, as race is. He forgets the example of gender. Just as some children are male and some female, some are born in the January-June period and others between July and December. Just as males and females develop different outlooks, so might children from the two chronological groups.

19. Jane Gross, "Big Grocery Chain Reaches Landmark Sex-Bias Accord," *New York Times*, December 17, 1993, pp. A1, B10.

20. Unpublished papers by Akiko Naono (1993) and Jacqueline Chu (1994), Economics Department, American University, Washington, D.C.

21. Lynne Duke, "Shoney's Bias Settlement Sends $105 Million Signal," *Washington Post*, February 5, 1993, pp. A1, A20.

22. *Employment and Earnings* (January 1995): table A-13.

23. Michael Fix and Raymond J. Struyk, eds., *Clear and Convincing Evidence: Measurement of Discrimination in America* (Washington, D.C.: Urban Institute Press, 1993).

24. Ibid.

25. Morin and Warden, "Americans Vent Anger."

26. For a compendium of all the texts of the relevant executive orders, see Jeffrey A. Norris and Salvador T. Perkins, *Developing Effective Affirmative Action Plans*, 4th ed. (Washington, D.C.: Employment Policy Foundation, 1993).

27. The Civil Rights Act, whose Title VII makes it illegal for employers to act so as to disadvantage people on account of their race, sex, religion, or national origin, does not explicitly require employers to implement effective affirmative action programs. It does, however, provide modest encouragement to them to do so. Title VII gives an aggrieved person or group who believe they have suffered discrimination the right to file a lawsuit against the employer in a federal court. The EEOC may also file suits against employers on behalf of individual employees or groups of employees. A firm may have a better chance of winning such a lawsuit if it has an affirmative action plan and is seen to be working toward achieving the plan's numerical goals.

28. See U.S. Department of Labor, OFCCP, "Companies Ineligible for Federal Contracts Under the Regulations of the Office of Federal Contract Compliance Programs," information sheet, September 29, 1994.

29. Table 2.3 is based on my tabulations from a computer tape containing employment information by race, sex, and occupational group sent in by all firms of 100 or more employees to

the EEOC. In addition to information on total employment in each firm, the tape carries information separately for each firm's larger workplaces. Information allowing a readout by name of firm for the largest government contractors was obtained by a Freedom of Information Act request to OFCCP. African Americans' share of jobs given in the table is the average for installations in metropolitan areas given on the tape.

30. Tomaskovic-Devey, *Gender and Racial Inequality*, pp. 66–67.

31. U.S. Bureau of the Census, *Statistical Abstract of the United States: 1994*, p. 546. Firms with government contracts worth at least $50,000 and having at least 50 employees are required to have affirmative action plans and to file reports on their employees by sex and race. All firms with at least 100 employees are required to file. However, firms with as few as fifteen employees are subject to Title VII of the Civil Rights Act. There is no pretense of monitoring the employment practices of the smaller firms.

32. With the possible exception of Xerox, all of these firms have received awards from OFCCP for "voluntary effort," according to the press packet prepared for distribution in 1995 by the agency.

33. The source is unpublished tabulations by Ann M. Beutel and Margaret Mooney Marini from data collected by the Survey Research Center at the University of Michigan. The number quoted includes those who answered "disagree" or "mostly disagree." See Beutel and Marini, "Gender and Values," *American Sociological Review* 60, no. 3 (June 1995): 436–48.

Chapter 3. How Exclusion Occurs

1. *Evans v. Sheraton Park Hotel*, 5 FEP Cases 393 (DDC 1972).

2. *Diaz v. Pan American World Airways, Inc.*, 442 F. 2d 385 (5th Cir. 1971). The case was brought by males who were being excluded from jobs as flight attendants.

3. Joleen Kirschenman and K. M. Neckerman, "We'd Love to Hire Them but . . . : The Meaning of Race for Employers," in *The Urban Underclass*, ed. Christopher Jencks and Paul E. Peterson (Washington, D.C.: Brookings Institution, 1991).

4. Susan D. Clayton and Faye J. Crosby, *Justice, Gender and Affirmative Action* (Ann Arbor: University of Michigan Press, 1992), pp. 73–78.

5. If the chances are 50–50 that the woman is superior to the man on any trait, and superiority on traits is assigned at random and independently, the woman will be better on all three traits one-eighth of the time, and the man will be better on all traits one-eighth of the time. In six-eighths of cases, the record will be mixed. In all of the cases with mixed records, respondents tend to judge the man's record more meritorious. As a result, the male will be judged better in seven-eighths of the pairs, whereas he should be judged better in only four-eighths of them.

6. Ian Ayres and Peter Siegelman, "Race and Gender Discrimination in Bargaining for a New Car," *American Economic Review* 85, no. 3 (June 1995): 304–21.

7. Sheryl B. Ball and Catherine C. Eckel, "Stars upon Thars: Status and Discrimination in Ultimatum Bargaining" (Blacksburg: Virginia Polytechnic Institute, Department of Economics, 1995).

8. Arthur Stinchcombe, *Information and Organizations* (Berkeley: University of California Press, 1990), pp. 243–44.

9. Donald Tomaskovic-Devey, *Gender and Racial Inequality at Work: The Sources and Consequences of Job Segregation* (Ithaca, N.Y.: ILR Press, 1993), pp. 161–62.

Chapter 4. Goals: Splitting the Pie

1. See Myra H. Strober, "Toward a General Theory of Occupational Sex Segregation: The Case of Public School Teaching," in *Sex Segregation in the Workplace: Trends, Explanations, Remedies,* ed. Barbara Reskin (Washington, D.C.: National Academy Press, 1984).

2. U.S. Code 206 (d) (1) (1970).

3. Jared Taylor, *Paved with Good Intentions* (New York: Carroll & Graf, 1992), p. 126.

4. *United Steelworkers of America, AFL-CIO v. Weber et al.,* 100 U.S. 193 (1979).

5. *Johnson v. Transportation Agency of Santa Clara County, Calif.,* 107 Sup. Ct. 1442 (1987).

6. The inclusion of women under the protection of the employment provisions of the act was originally introduced by an opponent in the hopes of making the bill less attractive. However, their inclusion was debated and passed on the merits. See Michael Evans Gold, "A Tale of Two Amendments: The Reasons Congress Added Sex to Title VII and Their Implication for the Issue of Comparable Worth," *Duquesne Law Review* 19 (Spring 1981): 453–77.

7. *Adarand Constructors, Inc. v. Federico Peña*, 115 S. Ct. 2097 (1995).

8. Ibid., p. 2121.

9. Irving Goffman, *Stigma: Notes on the Management of Spoiled Identity* (New York: Simon and Schuster, 1963).

10. M. V. Lee Badgett, "The Wage Effects of Sexual Orientation Discrimination," *Industrial and Labor Relations Review* 48, no. 4 (July 1995).

11. M. V. Lee Badgett, "Acting Affirmatively or Affirmative Action?: Constructing a Sexual Orientation Employment Policy" (College Park: University of Maryland School of Public Affairs, 1995).

12. This idea was suggested by Dr. David F. Duncan, Division of Biology and Medicine, Brown University, in an e-mail message to FEMMECON-L network, May 5, 1994.

Chapter 5. Thinking about Fairness

1. American Society for Personnel Administration, amicus curiae brief submitted to the Supreme Court, quoted in Justice William J. Brennan's majority opinion in *Johnson v. Transportation Agency of Santa Clara County, Calif.*, 107 Sup. Ct. 1442 (1987), p. 1457.

2. See Ivar Peterson, "Justice Officials Clarify Stand in Race-Based Case," *New York Times*, September 22, 1994, p. B6.

3. All material on Diane Joyce comes from the Supreme Court opinions in *Johnson v. Transportation Agency of Santa Clara County, Calif.*

4. Ibid., p. 1475.

5. David F. Duncan, Division of Biology and Medicine, Brown University, e-mail message to FEMECON-L network, May 5, 1994.

6. Jerome Karabel and David Karen, "Go to Harvard, Give Your Kid a Break," *New York Times*, December 8, 1990, p. 25.

7. The dean of the University of California Medical School—
   which figured in Alan Baake's reverse discrimination case that
   went to the Supreme Court—intervened each year in the
   admissions process on behalf of the children of friends and
   acquaintances.

8. See Barbara R. Bergmann, "Do Sports Really Make Money for
   the University?" *Academe* (January–February 1991): 28–30; and
   Murray Sperber, *College Sports Inc.: The Athletic Department vs.
   the University* (New York: Henry Holt and Co., 1990).

Chapter 6. Does Affirmative Action Hurt
Its Intended Beneficiaries?

1. *Adarand Constructors, Inc. v. Peña*, 115 S. Ct. 2097 (1995).

2. In the few case studies on hostile male behavior toward
   female workers, the men appeared to be trying to exclude
   competent women from traditionally male occupations. See
   Cynthia Cockburn, *In the Way of Women: Men's Resistance to Sex
   Equality in Organizations* (Ithaca, N.Y.: ILR Press, 1991).

3. See Donald Tomaskovic-Devey, *Gender and Racial Inequality at
   Work: The Sources and Consequences of Job Segregation* (Ithaca,
   N.Y.: ILR Press, 1993).

4. The source of this quotation is an e-mail communication.

5. Sandra Tangri, Martha R. Burt, and Eleanor B. Johnson, "Sexual Harassment at Work: Three Explanatory Models," *Journal
   of Social Issues* 38, no. 4 (1982): 33–54.

6. Margaret K. Webb, "Loyal Depositors Are Strongest Asset For
   One-Branch National Capital Bank," *Washington Post*, February 18, 1991, business sec., p. 8.

7. Shelby Steele, *The Content of Our Character* (New York: Harper Perennial, 1990), pp. 89–90.

8. Glen C. Loury, "Incentive Effects of Affirmative Action," in *Affirmative Action Revisited*, ed. Harold Orlans and June O'Neill, *Annals of the American Academy of Political and Social Science* 523 (September 1992): 21.

9. One Harvard economics professor subscribes to the view that recessions are caused by workers' simultaneous decisions to go on vacation. Another has attributed women's low wages to the fact that they need more supervision than men and are therefore more expensive to employ. Still another believes that the Social Security program has ruined our economy.

10. The fifty-two students were members of a group that had been assembled in Washington, D.C., for another purpose. They were therefore not a national random sample and represented only themselves.

11. Respondents were asked to choose a number from 1 (disagree strongly) to 5 (agree strongly). Those who picked 1 or 2 were tallied in the table as "disagreeing," those who picked 4 or 5 as "agreeing," and those who picked 3 as "undecided."

12. Shelby Steele, "How to Grow Extremists," *New York Times*, March 13, 1994, p. 17.

13. Ellis Cose, *The Rage of a Privileged Class* (New York: Harper-Collins, 1993).

Chapter 7. Opinions Pro and Con

1. See Thomas Sowell, *Preferential Policies: An International Perspective* (New York: William Morrow, 1990); and Shelby Steele,

The Content of Our Character (New York: Harper Perennial, 1990). Stephen Carter's *Reflections of an Affirmative Action Baby* (New York: Basic Books, 1991) expresses a somewhat more equivocal attitude.

2. Richard Morin and Sharon Warden, "Americans Vent Anger at Affirmative Action," *Washington Post*, March 24, 1995, p. 1.

3. Some respondents apparently viewed remedies 3, 4, and 5, the remedies that involved actual hiring, as mutually exclusive, and some checked off the more stringent ones without checking less stringent ones.

4. The probability of such a correlation occurring by chance is less than .001.

5. In a *Washington Post*–ABC poll that elicited a 75 percent negative response, the question referred to preference in "hiring, promotions, and college admissions." The inclusion of college admissions may have elevated the negative reaction because college admission offices are generally understood not to discriminate against African Americans, while sentiment is probably divided on whether any employers do. Morin and Warden, "Americans Vent Anger," p. 1.

6. Jeffrey A. Norris and Salvador T. Perkins, *Developing Effective Affirmative Action Plans*, 4th ed. (Washington, D.C.: Employment Policy Foundation, 1993), p. 10.

7. William B. Johnston and Arnold E. Packer, *Workforce 2000: Work and Workers for the Twenty-First Century* (Indianapolis: Hudson Institute, 1987), p. 95. The statement does not, of course, mean that by the year 2000 only 15 out of 100 workers will be white men. Nor, since it speaks of "net additions," as opposed to simply "additions," does it mean that only 15 per-

cent of the new young workers coming out of school and into the labor market will be white men. Properly interpreted, the statement means that the number of white men is currently growing, and that in the year 2000 there will actually be more of them available than there were in 1985. However, the white male share of the net additions would have to be on a par with their current share in the labor force, if the latter is to be maintained. The quoted statement, probably widely misunderstood, merely says that their share of net additions is far below their labor force share, and that their labor force share will as a result drop.

8. U.S. Bureau of the Census, *Statistical Abstract of the United States: 1992* (Washington, D.C.: U.S. Government Printing Office, 1992), p. 393.

Chapter 8. Alternatives to Affirmative Action

1. Such a substitution is consonant with the ideas of William J. Wilson, who has suggested that the problems of the African American community derive mainly from a high rate of poverty rather than from racial discrimination. See *The Truly Disadvantaged* (Chicago: University of Chicago Press, 1987).

2. U.S. Bureau of the Census, *Income, Poverty, and Valuation of Noncash Benefits: 1993*, Current Population Reports Series P60–188, (Washington, D.C.: U.S. Government Printing Office, 1995), p. xvi.

3. Material on this case and the USIA and DuPont cases is derived from Joan Biskupic, "After Nineteen Years, Racial Job-Bias Case Isn't over Yet," *Washington Post*, November 23, 1992, pp. 1, 12.

4. For an example of such a situation and a discussion of its limitations, see Barbara R. Bergmann, *The Economic Emergence of Women* (New York: Basic Books, 1986), pp. 76–81. In cases like the USIA suit, an expedited procedure for assessing damages to each individual might easily be used. In a sex discrimination case, such a procedure would involve first developing an estimate of how sex discrimination has affected the position and pay of the average woman in the class of complainants, allowing for differences between men and women in education, performance ratings, and years of experience. The calculation proposed is similar to that for calculating the "residual gap" in chap. 2. This would establish the total sum due the complainants. Second, the total award would be split up among the complainants by some simple rule of thumb. Such a procedure would take a month rather than half a decade to apply.

5. *Equal Employment Opportunity Commission, John R. Williams v. DuPont De Nemours and Co., Inc. and Neoprene Craftsmen's Union*, U.S. Ct. of Appeals for the Sixth Circuit, Slip Opinion, Oct. 5, 1981.

6. See U.S. Senate, Committee on Labor and Human Resources, *Federal Job Training Programs: The Need for Overhaul: Hearings before the Committee on Labor and Human Resources*, statement of James J. Heckman, January 1–12, 1995, pp. 260–72. These programs cost the federal government $24.8 billion in 1994; only 11 percent of them conducted studies of their effectiveness. See also *The Harassed Staffer's Guide to Employment and Training Policy* (Baltimore: Johns Hopkins University, Sar Levitan Center for Social Policy Studies, June 1995).

7. A 1993 *Wall Street Journal* article praised an apprenticeship program run by a modest-sized Virginia manufacturer of chain saws, lawn trimmers, and blowers. Starting in the late 1970s, the program turned thirty-six people into skilled crafts workers. Only two of the trainees were black; not a single one was a woman. Kevin G. Salwen, "The Cutting Edge; German-Owned Maker of Power Tools Finds Job Training Pays Off," *Wall Street Journal*, April 19, 1993, p. 1. A 1993 *Smithsonian* magazine story on apprenticeship mentioned in the text thirty-one trainees and trainers; not a single one was a woman. All of the several dozen people in the accompanying photographs were white. One picture did show one woman apprentice being taught pattern-making for women's clothes by a woman. E. Krester, "Germany Prepares Kids for Good Jobs; We Are Preparing Ours for Wendy's," *Smithsonian* 23 (March 1993): 44–50.

8. Sharon LaFraniere, "Testers to Probe Bias by Landlords," *Washington Post*, November 5, 1991, p. A19.

9. Richard J. Herrnstein and Charles Murray, *The Bell Curve: Intelligence and Class Structure in American Life* (New York: Free Press, 1994).

Index